P · E · R · F · E · C · T
CHICKEN
DISHES

P·E·R·F·E·C·T
CHICKEN
DISHES

BARNES
&NOBLE
BOOKS

NEW YORK

This edition published by Barnes & Noble, Inc.,
by arrangement with Dorling Kindersley Limited

2005 Barnes & Noble Books

M 10 9 8 7 6 5 4 3 2 1

ISBN 0-7607-6171-X

Created and Produced by
CARROLL & BROWN LTD
5 Lonsdale Road
London NW6 6RA

Editorial Director Jeni Wright
Copy Editor Norma MacMillan
Art Editor Mary Staples
Designers Lyndel Donaldson
Wendy Rogers
Lucy de Rosa
Lisa Webb

Color reproduction by Colourscan, Singapore
Printed and bound by Star Standard, Singapore

CONTENTS

PERFECT CHICKEN

Welcome to **Perfect Chicken**. This volume is designed to be one of the simplest, most informative cookbooks you'll ever own. It is the closest I can come to sharing my techniques for cooking my own favorite recipes without actually being with you in the kitchen looking over your shoulder.

Equipment and ingredients often determine whether or not you can cook a particular dish, so **Perfect Chicken**

illustrates everything you need at the beginning of each recipe. You'll see at a glance how long a recipe takes to cook, how many servings it makes, what the finished dish looks like, and how much preparation can be done ahead. When you start to cook, you'll find the preparation and cooking are organized into easy-to-follow steps. Each stage is color-coded and everything is shown in photographs with brief text to go with each step. You will never be in doubt about what it is you are doing, why you are doing it, or how it should look.

EQUIPMENT

·INGREDIENTS

🍽 SERVES 4-6   🥣 WORK TIME 25-35 MINUTES   🍲 COOKING TIME 20-30 MINUTES

I've also included helpful hints and ideas under "Anne Says." These may list an alternative ingredient or piece of equipment, or sometimes the reason for using a certain method is explained, or there is advice on mastering a particular technique. Similarly, if there is a crucial stage in a recipe when things can go wrong, I've included some warnings called "Take Care."

Many of the photographs are annotated to pinpoint why certain pieces of equipment work best, or how the food should look at that stage of cooking. Because presentation is so important, a picture of the finished dish and serving suggestions are at the end of each recipe.

Thanks to all this information, you can't go wrong. I'll be with you every step of the way. So please, come with me into the kitchen to look, cook, and create some perfect chicken dishes.

WHY CHICKEN?

Chicken is so versatile that mastering a range of chicken recipes is one of the most useful things for a cook. Sold in so many forms, chicken can be dressed up to grace the most elegant dinner table or simply cooked to provide the basis of innumerable everyday meals. Chicken can be prepared in many different ways, delicious on its own, cooked in a sauce, or combined with all sorts of vegetables and even with shellfish. Traditional accompaniments add even more character, differing from country to country and often depending on the cooking method employed.

RECIPE CHOICE

Practically every country in the world has a favorite chicken dish, and my selection of recipes attempts to marry traditional cooking styles and ingredients with the wide variety of chicken cuts available. Here's an overview of the chicken classics old and new that you will find in this book. To make your choice easy, they are grouped by type – whole birds, pieces, breasts, or cooked meat.

WHOLE BIRDS

A whole bird, simply roasted, is widely served throughout America and Europe, and the French method of roasting chicken in a fairly high heat guarantees the most successful result. My four recipes use this method. *Chicken Château du Feÿ*: Bird is stuffed with herbs and roasted with butter. *Roast Chicken with Lemon*: A whole lemon gives additional character. *Roast Chicken with Lemon and Herb Butter*: Bird is "self-basted" with flavored butter under the skin. *Roast Chicken with Garlic*: Roasted garlic cloves add flavor and thicken the sauce.

A full-size chicken can also be poached. *Yorkshire Chicken with Stuffed Prunes*: Chicken is poached with breadcrumb-stuffed prunes and a rich velouté cream sauce. *Chicken in Parsley Sauce*: Velouté sauce is flavored with plenty of parsley and lemon.

If flattened to cook evenly, a whole chicken can be broiled. *Broiled Chicken with Garlic Herb Butter*: Split and flattened, the chicken is spread with garlic herb butter and broiled. Small-sized chickens or Rock Cornish hens are also delicious broiled. *Broiled Baby Chickens with Mushroom Sauce*: Mustard adds flavor to a tasty rich mushroom sauce.

These small chickens are delicious pot roasted, too. *Chicken en Cocotte with Lemon and Parmesan*: Baby chickens are cooked in a covered pot with lemon and served with a zesty sauce. *Chicken with Thyme*: Sprigs of fresh thyme add flavor to chicken baked in a pot. *Chicken en Cocotte with Juniper Berries and Wild Mushrooms*: Earthy juniper berries and wild mushrooms are natural partners for chicken. *Stuffed Baby Chickens with Grapes*: Baby chickens with couscous stuffing are served with red or green grapes and a port wine sauce. *Stuffed Baby Chickens with Chili Sauce*: Fiery harissa in tomato sauce adds spice to these couscous-stuffed little birds.

CHICKEN PIECES

A whole chicken, cut up, provides four, six, or eight breast and leg pieces, or pieces can be bought pre-packaged. They can be cooked in a number of ways. Sautés involve browning the chicken pieces then cooking them in their own juices with the addition of various liquids, other flavorings and occasionally, other ingredients. *Sauté of Chicken with Paprika*: A Hungarian accent is given with paprika, red pepper, and sour cream. *Szechuan Pepper Chicken*: Sautéed chicken goes Oriental with spicy Chinese pepper. *Sauté of Chicken with Dark Beer*: Stout and a jigger of gin inspire this recipe. *Sauté of Chicken with Mussels*: The saltiness of mussels provides the flavor, green beans add color. *Chicken with Clams*: Clams are delicious when combined with chicken.

Two dishes that depend on frying. *Southern Fried Chicken with Pan Gravy*: The unbeatable American classic. *Bacon-Fried Chicken*: Bacon fat adds piquancy to this fried chicken.

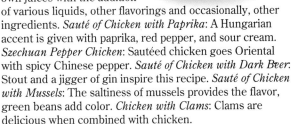

From North Africa come two casseroles that require diffused heat. *Moroccan Chicken Baked with Spices:* Cinnamon, ginger, and saffron highlight the apricots and honey in this classic dish. *Moroccan Chicken with Eggplant:* Chicken with an offbeat combination of eggplant and lemon, coriander and cumin giving it a highly seasoned taste.

Chicken pieces can also stand up to more prolonged cooking. *Brunswick Stew:* A rich stew with lima beans and corn kernels thickened with potato. *Chicken With Kidney Beans and Kielbasa:* Red beans and garlic sausage make this stew a hearty meal. *Chicken Stew Basquaise:* Tomatoes and roasted bell peppers produce the classic Basquaise flavor.

Three of my dishes improve by being prepared ahead. *Chicken in Red Wine:* Classic "Coq au Vin." *Chicken in White Wine:* Medium-dry white wine is the base for this light sauce with onions and mushrooms. *Chicken in Beaujolais:* This light, fruity, red wine is delicious with chicken.

Chicken pieces are ideal for eating with the fingers. *Deviled Drumsticks with Warm Potato Salad:* A piquant spice mixture for barbecued chicken legs, great for outdoors. *Deviled Chicken Wings:* Perfect food for a crowd.

And less expensive cuts can make unusual fare. *Broiled Chicken Thighs in Yogurt:* Yogurt tenderizes the chicken and creates a spicy sauce. *Broiled Chicken Thighs with Yogurt and Honey:* Tangy and sweet, this sauce broils well.

CHICKEN BREASTS

Tender all-white-meat chicken breasts are the most expensive form of chicken to buy, but boning them yourself can make them more economical. *Chicken in a Paper Case with Julienne Vegetables:* These chicken breasts are great for a small dinner party. *Chicken in a Paper Case with Bell Peppers:* Sweet bell peppers accompany chicken breasts baked in paper cases.

Two easy stir-fry dishes that use chicken meat cut into fine slices. *Oriental Stir-Fried Chicken:* A quick and tasty stir-fry. *Sweet and Sour Stir-Fried Chicken:* Pineapple adds Hawaiian tang to this stir-fry.

Chicken breast meat is ideal for kebabs, marinated cubes threaded on a skewer and grilled. *Indonesian Chicken Kebabs:* A delectable snack of spicy chicken served with a peanut sauce. *Vietnamese Chicken Kebabs:* Ginger and lemon grass give a special flavor to these kebabs.

Poached chicken breast meat with contrasting filling on a pool of sauce is great for special occasions. *Pinwheel Chicken with Herbs and Goat Cheese:* Pretty pinwheel rolls are just right for an elegant dinner. *Pinwheel Chicken Italienne:* Parma ham and fontina cheese add Italian panache to pinwheel chicken breasts.

Finely ground breast meat is versatile for shaping and whisking into mixtures. *Ground Chicken Cutlets:* A Russian recipe with a crunchy coating. *Cocktail Pojarski:* Great, do-ahead snacks for a cocktail party. *Cold Chicken and Ham Pie:* A grand savory pie perfect for a picnic. *Hot Chicken and Ham Pie:* Zesty horseradish sauce accompanies this hot meat pie. *Chicken Mousse with Madeira Butter Sauce:* Fluffy chicken mousse served with a luxurious butter sauce. *Cold Chicken Mousse with Tomato Coulis and Mint:* Ideal for a festive summer lunch.

COOKED CHICKEN MEAT

Chicken is a favorite for salads both hot and cold. Start with home-cooked roast chicken or buy it ready cooked. *Chicken with Curry Dressing and Saffron Rice:* A spicy variation on chicken salad. *Chicken with Tarragon Dressing and Rice:* The sweet aroma of tarragon is a classic partner for chicken. *Tex-Mex Chicken Salad:* Tomatoes, corn, and peppers form a sunburst of color. *Cobb Salad:* A California favorite with blue cheese, bacon, and avocado.

Use cooked chicken, too, as a filling for hot pies. *Chicken Pot Pies with Herb Crust:* Pastry biscuits top cooked chicken and diced vegetables. *Large Chicken Pot Pie:* A warming meal for a cold winter's day.

EQUIPMENT

Cooking chicken requires very little specialized equipment and usually standard tools can be substituted.

A chef's knife or poultry shears is needed to cut up a chicken and a boning knife is useful when boning breasts or removing a tendon. All knives should be sharpened regularly and stored carefully to prevent dulling.

A trussing needle and string may be necessary to tie a whole bird into shape. Metal skewers can be used for trussing, as well as for holding chicken kebabs and flattened chicken pieces down for broiling. Bamboo skewers are attractive for serving kebabs, but they must be soaked in water to keep them from scorching during cooking. A meat grinder or food processor is important for ground chicken dishes; the meat tends to jam in a blender.

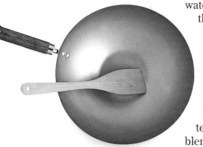

INGREDIENTS

Chicken goes with an astonishingly wide variety of ingredients.

Butter is essential for adding a crisp golden skin to roast chicken but in many other recipes olive oil, and flavored nut oils, are taking its place.

A full range of fresh herbs – basil, tarragon, rosemary, oregano, thyme, chives – make a natural marriage with chicken, not to mention the often neglected common parsley. The neutral flavor of chicken blends equally well with spices such as nutmeg, cinnamon, curry powder, allspice, and the zesty impact of chili pepper. Almost all vegetables complement chicken, from roots such as carrot and onion to greens such as spinach, plus tomatoes, bell peppers and the entire edible mushroom family. Shellfish combined with chicken adds salty flavor, a handy seasoning for the mild meat.

As for wine, many of the most famous chicken classics rely on red wine, white wine, and fortified wines such as sherry and Marsala for their character.

Chicken is one of the most economical sources of high-quality protein and, cooked without its skin, is lower in calories than most other meats. Light meat contains less fat and less cholesterol than dark, and chicken breast meat can be used in any recipe calling for pieces.

My recipes, like all traditional French cooking, use butter and salt as standard ingredients. If you are concerned to cut calories and fats, you can substitute polyunsaturated margarine or mono- and polyunsaturated oils, but the results will not be as successful. Nonstick cooking spray and a teaspoon or two of oil, preferably in a non-stick skillet, may work for the sauté dishes. I usually don't indicate amounts for salt, as this should be to taste only, and the herbs and spices I use should make the dishes flavorsome without too much salt.

TECHNIQUES

If you master just a few techniques for working with chicken, you will be able to tackle a wide variety of recipes. For instance, removing the tendon from a chicken breast prevents shrinkage and makes the meat tender for serving. Cutting out the wishbone makes a whole bird easy to carve, while trussing ensures even cooking and an attractive shape.

Chickens are often sold already cut up into pieces, but if you cut up a chicken yourself, the pieces will be meaty and of an even size, while the bones from trimming can be used for making chicken stock.

Carving a whole cooked bird, cutting neat slices of both white and dark meat, has long been an art. Boning a cooked bird, discarding the skin so only the meat is left, is yet another possibility, often needed for chicken salad.

As with the other volumes in this series, there are techniques for preparing ingredients other than chicken. You will find how to chop herbs; how to peel, seed, and chop tomatoes; how to peel and chop garlic, chop shallots, and slice or chop onions; how to clean and quarter or slice mushrooms; how to prepare and slice an avocado; how to cut julienne vegetables; and how to roast, seed, and slice bell peppers, as well as make a bouquet garni and vinaigrette dressing.

CHICKEN
CHATEAU DU FEY

🍽 SERVES 4-6 🥣 WORK TIME 20-30 MINUTES 🍲 COOKING TIME 1-1¼ HOURS

EQUIPMENT

carving board

strainer

small knife

chef's knife*

paper towels

2-pronged fork

large
metal spoon

wooden spoon

aluminum foil

2 metal skewers

roasting pan
just large enough
to hold chicken

*carving knife can also be used

Here is a staple of our dinners at home in Burgundy – a classic roast chicken without a stuffing but with herbs inside for flavor. Its simplicity will make it one of your favorites, too. The butter used in cooking the chicken goes into the gravy so the more butter you use, the richer the gravy will be! You can present the chicken whole, as shown here, to be carved at the table. Or, if it is easier, carve it in the kitchen. Roast potatoes – crisp on the outside and tender within – are a perfect accompaniment to the juicy chicken.

GETTING AHEAD

There's really no way to reheat a roast chicken satisfactorily. However, the bird can be kept warm at least 30 minutes by wrapping it loosely in foil as soon as it comes from the oven.

SHOPPING LIST

1	roasting chicken, weighing 4-4½ lbs
	salt and pepper
2-3	large sprigs of fresh thyme
2-3	large sprigs of fresh rosemary
1	bay leaf
¼ - ⅓ cup	butter
2 cups	chicken stock

INGREDIENTS

chicken

chicken stock   butter

fresh
rosemary

bay leaf   fresh
thyme

ORDER OF WORK

1 PREPARE THE
   CHICKEN

2 ROAST THE
   CHICKEN

3 MAKE THE GRAVY

1 PREPARE THE CHICKEN

1 Heat the oven to 425° F. Wipe the inside of the chicken clean with paper towels.

2 Remove the wishbone from the chicken (see box, below left). Season the chicken inside and out with salt and pepper. Put the herbs inside the chicken.

ANNE SAYS
"Tarragon, oregano, or any fresh aromatic herb can be used instead of the thyme or rosemary. Dried herbs are much less satisfactory."

3 Set the bird breast-side up and push the legs back and down. Insert one skewer near the knee joint and push it through the bird and out through the other leg.

HOW TO REMOVE A WISHBONE

1 Fold back the neck skin of the chicken. With the point of a small knife, loosen the wishbone.

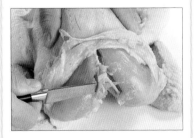

2 Remove the wishbone. Also remove any fat.

ANNE SAYS
"Without the wishbone, the breast meat is easy to carve into thin slices."

4 Turn the bird over so it is back-side up. Pull the neck skin over the neck cavity and tuck the wing tips over it.

5 Push the second skewer through both sections of one wing and into the neck skin. Continue under the backbone of the bird to the other side. Push the skewer through the second wing in the same way, through both wing bones.

6 Turn the chicken breast-side up again. It is now ready for cooking.

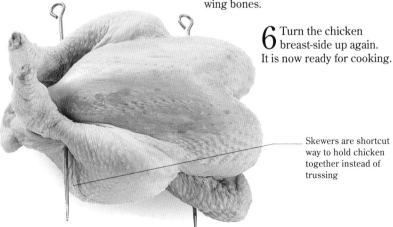

Skewers are shortcut way to hold chicken together instead of trussing

2 ROAST THE CHICKEN

1 Put the chicken in the roasting pan, breast-side up. Cut the butter into slices and arrange them on the chicken breast.

ANNE SAYS

"Adding butter to the chicken in this way enriches the meat and gives a characteristic golden color to the skin. The quantity is up to you but ¼ cup is a minimum."

Sturdy metal roasting pan has low sides so oven heat can reach sides of bird

HOW TO TEST A CHICKEN FOR DONENESS

A chicken is thoroughly cooked when the juices from the cavity run clear. To test, lift the bird with the 2-pronged fork and tip it so you can see the color of the juices that run out of the cavity into the roasting pan.

2 Roast the chicken in the heated oven for 1-1¼ hours, basting it every 10-15 minutes with the juices in the pan.

ANNE SAYS

"Regular basting is the key to a juicy bird with well-browned, crisp skin."

3 To keep the meat moist, turn the chicken onto its breast after it starts to brown. Return it breast-side up about 15 minutes before the end of cooking. Transfer the chicken to the carving board and cover with foil to keep warm while making the gravy.

3 MAKE THE GRAVY

1 Add the stock to the roasting pan and boil over high heat, stirring to dissolve the pan juices. Continue boiling until the gravy is thoroughly reduced and concentrated.

ANNE SAYS
"Hard boiling will emulsify the butter and fat from roasting and thicken the gravy slightly."

Use conical strainer when pouring gravy to avoid spills

2 Taste for seasoning, then strain the gravy carefully through the conical strainer into a gravy boat or serving bowl.

🍽 TO SERVE
Present the chicken whole, or carve it (see box, page 14) in the kitchen and serve on individual plates. Serve the gravy separately.

Fresh herbs such as thyme, rosemary, and bay leaf give an attractive touch

Potatoes, roasted in oil and butter, are an ideal accompaniment

HOW TO CARVE A COOKED CHICKEN

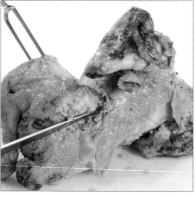

1 Remove the skewers. With a chef's knife, cut down between the leg and the body.

2 Turn the bird on its side and cut close to the backbone, leaving the "oyster" meat attached to the thigh.

3 Turn the bird again onto its back. Twist the leg sharply outward to break the joint, then cut through it and pull the leg from the body. Repeat the procedure to remove the other leg.

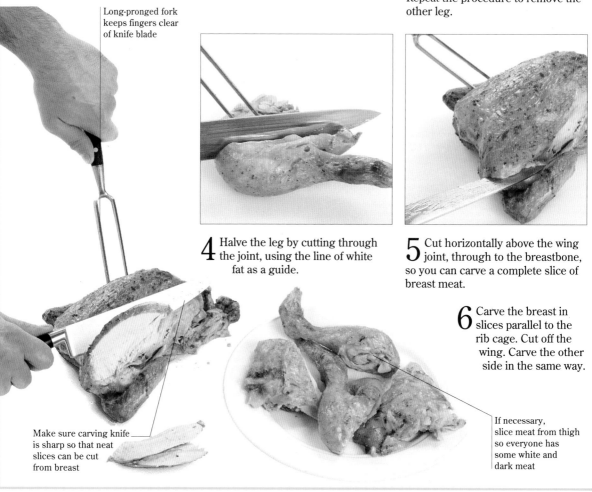

Long-pronged fork keeps fingers clear of knife blade

4 Halve the leg by cutting through the joint, using the line of white fat as a guide.

5 Cut horizontally above the wing joint, through to the breastbone, so you can carve a complete slice of breast meat.

6 Carve the breast in slices parallel to the rib cage. Cut off the wing. Carve the other side in the same way.

Make sure carving knife is sharp so that neat slices can be cut from breast

If necessary, slice meat from thigh so everyone has some white and dark meat

ROAST CHICKEN
WITH LEMON

Replace the thyme, rosemary, and bay leaf in Chicken Château du Feÿ with a lemon. If you can get an unsprayed, unwaxed lemon, so much the better.

1 Scrub the lemon, then roll it on a work surface to help release the juices. Prick it with a fork, place inside the chicken, and roast the bird as directed.
2 When making the gravy, stir in a squeeze of lemon juice before straining it.
3 For serving, cut a fresh lemon into neat slices and use to decorate the chicken.

ROAST CHICKEN WITH LEMON AND
HERB BUTTER

1 Prepare the chicken as directed through step 2 of Chicken Château du Feÿ.
2 Finely grate the zest of 1 lemon. Strip the leaves from 2-3 sprigs of fresh thyme and 2-3 sprigs of fresh rosemary. Cut the leaves into small pieces, then chop them finely. Beat the lemon zest and herbs into ¼ cup butter.
3 In step 3 of the main recipe, lift the breast skin with your fingers and carefully ease it away from the meat; spread the flesh with the butter. Continue as directed in the main recipe, from the beginning of step 3.

ROAST CHICKEN
WITH GARLIC

A garlic lover's dream: unpeeled cloves of garlic are roasted with the chicken, then crushed to thicken the sauce. Surprisingly, once the garlic has been cooked, it has a mellow, sweet taste.

1 Prepare and roast the chicken as directed in Chicken Château du Feÿ.
2 Separate the cloves from 1 head of garlic; do not peel them. Spread the garlic cloves in the roasting pan around the chicken when you first baste it, 10-15 minutes after it goes into the oven.
3 Make the gravy as directed, and when straining, crush the garlic against the side of the strainer to extract the pulp.
4 If you like, prepare a roasted garlic garnish: Slice the top off 4-6 heads of garlic (1 per person), drizzle with a little olive oil, and arrange in an oiled baking dish. Roast with the chicken, about 45 minutes. To eat, squeeze out the soft cloves of garlic.

DEVILED DRUMSTICKS WITH WARM POTATO SALAD

 SERVES 4 🥣 WORK TIME 20-25 MINUTES 🍲 COOKING TIME 35-40 MINUTES

EQUIPMENT

chef's knife

small knife

bowls

pastry brush

metal spoon

whisk

saucepans

colander

chopping board

2-pronged fork

aluminum foil

ANNE SAYS
"*Four small Cornish hens or baby chickens, one per person, can be used in place of the small chickens. They will need only about 25 minutes cooking and should be served whole.*"

These spicy chicken drumsticks are archetypal barbecue fare, and are excellent cooked on the charcoal grill. Accompany them with corn on the cob. For the potato salad, look for baby potatoes, or firm large potatoes which will hold their shape when boiled.

SHOPPING LIST

8	chicken drumsticks
	vegetable oil for broiler rack
	For the devil mixture
1/2 cup	butter
2 tbsp	mango chutney
2 tbsp	tomato paste or ketchup
2 tbsp	Worcestershire sauce
1 tsp	ground nutmeg
1/2 tsp	anchovy paste
	salt and pepper
	cayenne or Tabasco
	For the potato salad
2 tbsp	red wine vinegar
1/4 - 1/2 tsp	Dijon-style mustard
6 tbsp	vegetable oil
a few	sprigs of parsley
a few	fresh chives
1 1/2 lbs	baby potatoes, or 4 large firm potatoes, peeled

INGREDIENTS

butter

chicken drumsticks

tomato paste

mango chutney

anchovy paste

Dijon-style mustard

cayenne

fresh chives

vegetable oil

parsley   potatoes

ground nutmeg

red wine vinegar   Worcestershire sauce

ORDER OF WORK

1 **MAKE THE DEVIL MIXTURE**

2 **MAKE THE POTATO SALAD**

3 **PREPARE AND BROIL THE CHICKEN**

1 MAKE THE DEVIL MIXTURE

1 First, melt the butter in a small saucepan. Chop any large pieces of fruit in the chutney.

2 Put the chutney in a small bowl and add the remaining devil mixture ingredients, with a pinch of cayenne or dash of Tabasco, and the melted butter. Mix together well, using the metal spoon. Taste for seasoning.

Spices mixed with liquids make tasty coating for chicken

2 MAKE THE POTATO SALAD

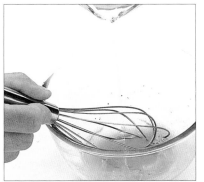

1 Make a vinaigrette dressing (see page 36) with the vinegar, mustard, oil, and a pinch each of salt and pepper.

2 With the chef's knife, chop the parsley and chives.

3 If using large potatoes, cut each one into 2-3 pieces. Leave baby potatoes unpeeled. Put the potatoes in a medium saucepan of salted water and bring to a boil. Cover and simmer until tender when pierced with the point of the small knife, 15-20 minutes.

4 Drain the potatoes thoroughly in the colander, then cut into ³⁄₈-inch-thick slices. Transfer them to a large bowl.

Let potatoes cool a little before slicing

5 While the potatoes are still warm, add the chopped herbs and pour on the vinaigrette dressing; mix gently. Cover with foil and keep warm.

HOW TO CHOP HERBS

1 Strip the leaves or sprigs from the stems. Pile the leaves or sprigs on a chopping board.

2 With a very sharp chef's knife, cut the leaves or sprigs into small pieces.

ANNE SAYS

"When chopping a large quantity of herbs or sprigs of herbs such as parsley, hold them together in a bunch with your other hand while chopping."

3 Holding the tip of the blade against the board and rocking the handle of the knife up and down, chop until the herbs are coarse or fine, as you wish.

! TAKE CARE !

Do not chop delicate herbs such as basil and tarragon too finely because they bruise easily.

3 PREPARE AND BROIL THE CHICKEN

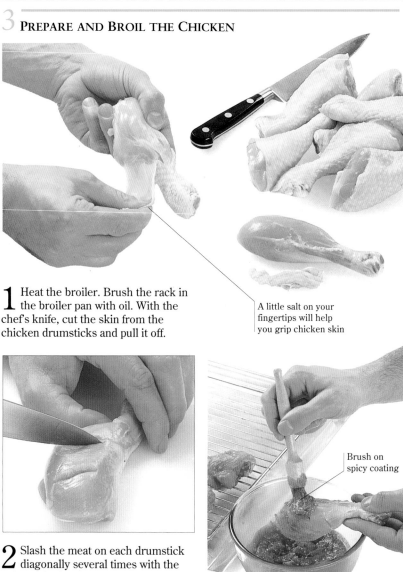

A little salt on your fingertips will help you grip chicken skin

1 Heat the broiler. Brush the rack in the broiler pan with oil. With the chef's knife, cut the skin from the chicken drumsticks and pull it off.

2 Slash the meat on each drumstick diagonally several times with the point of the knife.

Brush on spicy coating

3 Brush some of the devil mixture onto each drumstick, working the mixture well into the cuts in the meat. Arrange the drumsticks on the oiled broiler rack.

4 Broil the chicken drumsticks 3-4 inches from the heat, turning them once during cooking.

DEVILED CHICKEN WINGS

This is a version of Buffalo Chicken Wings, popular as tavern food with a cool glass of beer.

1 Prepare the devil mixture as directed in the main recipe for drumsticks.
2 Substitute 12-14 chicken wings for the drumsticks. Cut off the wing tips and discard them, then coat the wings and cook as directed.
3 Omit the potato salad.

5 During cooking, baste the chicken drumsticks frequently with the remaining devil mixture and any pan juices. Cook until they are well browned and tender, about 10-12 minutes on each side.

🍽 **TO SERVE**
Arrange the warm potato salad on individual plates, with the drumsticks alongside.

— **GETTING AHEAD** —
The drumsticks and salad can be prepared a day ahead and kept, covered, in the refrigerator. The drumsticks can be served either hot or cold. To reheat, wrap in foil and warm in a 350°F oven about 10 minutes.

Devil coating
on drumsticks can be
as hot as you like

MOROCCAN CHICKEN BAKED WITH SPICES

¶Ⓞ¶ SERVES 4   🥣 WORK TIME 10-15 MINUTES   ♨ COOKING TIME 1½ HOURS

EQUIPMENT

tajine*

poultry shears

saucepan

chef's knife

2-pronged fork

strainer

bowls

chopping board

large metal spoon

slotted spoon

*heavy casserole (preferably earthenware) with lid can also be used

ANNE SAYS
"*Small chickens are typical of Morocco, but you can easily substitute a larger one and cut it into 6 pieces. Larger chickens will require a slightly longer cooking time.*"

This is a version of the classic Moroccan "tajine," a mixture of chicken, fruit, and spices baked under a conical earthenware cover. Any heavy casserole can be substituted, preferably of earthenware to diffuse the heat. Instead of cutting up the chicken yourself, you may prefer to buy it in 4 pieces.

GETTING AHEAD
The chicken can be baked up to 3 days ahead and refrigerated, or it can be frozen. Warm it in a 350°F oven 20-30 minutes before serving.

INGREDIENTS

onions

chicken

dried apricots   parsley sprigs

honey

tomatoes

saffron

olive oil

ground cinnamon   ground ginger

SHOPPING LIST

1	chicken, weighing 3-3½ lbs
	saffron
3-4 tbsp	boiling water
a few	sprigs of parsley
1 lb	tomatoes
6	onions
½ cup	dried apricots
2 tbsp	honey
2 tsp	ground cinnamon
1 tsp	ground ginger
	salt and pepper
½ cup	olive oil

ORDER OF WORK

1 CUT UP THE CHICKEN

2 PREPARE OTHER INGREDIENTS

3 COOK THE CHICKEN

1 CUT UP THE CHICKEN

Make sure knife is sharp and positioned at joint

1 Using the chef's knife, cut down between the leg joint and body on one side. Twist the bone sharply outward to break the joint, then cut through it and pull the leg from the body. Repeat this procedure for the other leg.

2 Slit the chicken closely along both sides of the breastbone to loosen the meat, then split the breastbone with the poultry shears.

3 Turn the bird over onto its breast and cut the rib bones and backbone from the breast in one piece, leaving the wing joints attached to the breast. The 2 breast halves of the bird are now divided.

2 PREPARE OTHER INGREDIENTS

1 Put a large pinch of saffron into a small bowl. Spoon on the boiling water. Set aside to soak.

2 Chop the parsley. Peel, seed, and chop the tomatoes.

Chop tomatoes coarsely with sharp knife

ANNE SAYS
"There is no need to peel tomatoes with thin tender skin, but do remove the seeds and surrounding juice because they would make the dish watery."

HOW TO SLICE AN ONION

1 Peel the onion and trim the top. Cut the onion lengthwise in half, from top to root.

ANNE SAYS
"Leaving the root on helps hold the onion together during slicing."

2 Put one half cut-side down on the chopping board. Holding the onion firmly, cut it crosswise into slices, starting where the top has been trimmed and guiding the knife with your bent fingers. Discard the root when you reach it. Repeat with the other half of the onion.

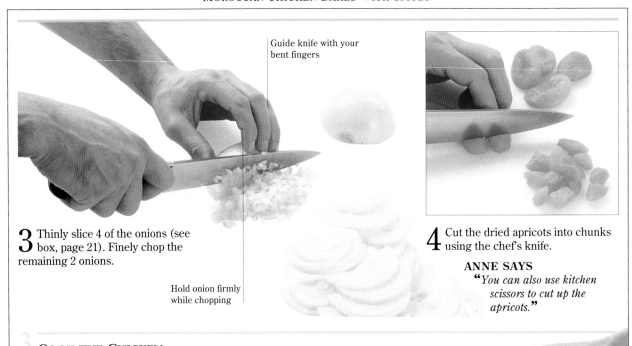

Guide knife with your
bent fingers

3 Thinly slice 4 of the onions (see
box, page 21). Finely chop the
remaining 2 onions.

Hold onion firmly
while chopping

4 Cut the dried apricots into chunks
using the chef's knife.

ANNE SAYS
*"You can also use kitchen
scissors to cut up the
apricots."*

3 COOK THE CHICKEN

Spread mixture in
even layer over
tomatoes

1 Heat the oven to 350° F. Put the
chicken in the tajine. Cover with
the sliced onions, then with the
chopped tomatoes.

2 Mix the chopped onions, saffron
and its liquid, dried apricots,
honey, cinnamon, ginger, chopped
parsley, salt, and pepper together in a
bowl. Add the olive oil. Spoon the
mixture over the chicken.

MOROCCAN CHICKEN WITH EGGPLANT

3 Cover and bake in the heated oven until the chicken is tender when pierced with the 2-pronged fork, about 1½ hours.

Conical lid of tajine seals in cooking juices

🍲 TO SERVE

Taste the sauce for seasoning. Serve the chicken and sauce straight from the tajine onto individual plates.

ANNE SAYS

"*If you use another type of earthenware pot or heavy casserole, be sure the lid fits tightly.*"

1 Cut up the chicken and prepare the onions and tomatoes as for Moroccan Chicken Baked with Spices.

2 Cut 1 medium eggplant (about ½ lb) in half and slice it. Put the slices in a colander, sprinkle with coarse salt, press down with a plate, and leave to drain 30 minutes; wipe the slices dry with paper towels.

3 Trim the ends from 1 lemon and cut it into wedges.

4 Put the chicken pieces in a casserole and cover with the sliced onions, tomatoes, eggplant, and lemon wedges.

5 In a bowl, mix together the chopped onions, 1 garlic clove, finely chopped, ½ cup olive oil, 2 tsp ground cumin, 2 tsp ground coriander, salt, pepper, and a few sprigs of fresh coriander (cilantro), chopped. Spoon this mixture over the chicken.

6 Sprinkle ¾ cup whole pitted black or green olives over the chicken and cook as directed. Remove the lemon wedges before serving.

Couscous stuffing with almonds, used in the recipe for Stuffed Baby Chickens with Grapes (see page 94), is the perfect accompaniment

INDONESIAN CHICKEN KEBABS

Saté Ayam, Bumbu Saté

🍽 SERVES 6 AS A MAIN COURSE　🥣 WORK TIME 15-20 MINUTES*　🍲 COOKING TIME 8-10 MINUTES

EQUIPMENT

food processor**

frying pan

chef's knife

pastry brush

boning knife

wooden spoon

metal spoons

rubber spatula

bowls

chopping board

18 bamboo skewers***

plastic wrap

medium saucepan

shallow dish

**blender can also be used
***metal skewers can also be used

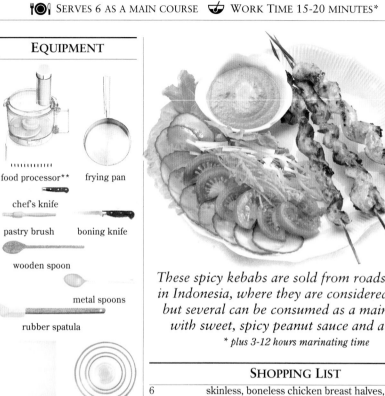

These spicy kebabs are sold from roadside stalls in Indonesia, where they are considered snacks, but several can be consumed as a main course with sweet, spicy peanut sauce and a salad.
* *plus 3-12 hours marinating time*

SHOPPING LIST

6	skinless, boneless chicken breast halves, total weight about 3 lbs
	For the marinade
3	shallots
2	garlic cloves
1/2 tsp	chili powder
2 tsp	ground coriander
2 tsp	ground ginger
3 tbsp	soy sauce
2 tbsp	distilled white vinegar
2 tbsp	vegetable oil
	For the peanut sauce
1 1/2 tbsp	vegetable oil
1 1/2 cups	shelled, skinned raw peanuts
1/2	medium onion
1	garlic clove
1/2 tsp	dried hot red pepper flakes
2 tsp	ground ginger
1 tsp	brown sugar
1 1/2 tbsp	lemon juice
1 1/2 cups	hot water
	salt and pepper

INGREDIENTS

chicken breast halves

shallots

garlic cloves

soy sauce

onion

shelled, skinned raw peanuts

lemon juice

ground coriander

chili powder

ground ginger

dried hot red pepper flakes

brown sugar

vegetable oil

distilled white vinegar

ORDER OF WORK

1　PREPARE AND MARINATE THE CHICKEN

2　MAKE THE PEANUT SAUCE

3　PREPARE AND COOK THE KEBABS

PREPARE AND MARINATE THE CHICKEN

1 Remove the tendon from each chicken breast half. Separate the fillet from each breast by lifting the end of the fillet and pulling it toward you. With the chef's knife, cut each fillet in half lengthwise. Cut each breast into 7 thin strips on the diagonal, the same size as the strips of fillet.

2 Finely chop the shallots (see box, right). Finely chop the garlic. Put all the marinade ingredients in a large bowl. Mix together with a metal spoon.

Marinade ingredients give delicious flavor and moistness to chicken

3 Add the chicken strips and mix until well coated with the marinade. Cover with plastic wrap and refrigerate at least 3 hours or up to 12 hours.

HOW TO CHOP A SHALLOT

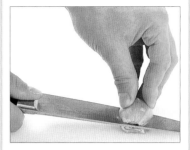

1 If necessary, separate the shallot into sections at the root. Peel each section and set it flat-side down on a chopping board. Holding the shallot section steady with your fingers, slice it horizontally toward the root, leaving the slices attached at the root end. For a standard chop, make slices about $1/8$-inch thick; for a fine chop, make slices as thin as possible.

2 Slice vertically through the shallot, again leaving the root end uncut.

3 Cut across the shallot to make fine dice. Continue chopping the shallot until very fine, if necessary. The root end may be reserved for stock.

2 MAKE THE PEANUT SAUCE

1 Heat the oil in the frying pan. Add the peanuts and cook, stirring constantly, until browned, 3-5 minutes. Transfer the peanuts to the food processor.

Toast peanuts to enhance their nutty flavor

Stir nuts while browning so they do not stick and burn

2 Cut the onion into pieces and add to the food processor with the garlic, hot pepper flakes, ginger, brown sugar, and lemon juice. Purée the mixture until very smooth, scraping the bowl with the spatula as necessary.

ANNE SAYS
"If the mixture is difficult to process smoothly, add a little hot water."

3 Blend in the hot water, adding enough to make a pourable sauce that coats the back of a spoon. Transfer the sauce to the saucepan, heat to boiling, and simmer 2 minutes, stirring constantly. Season to taste. Remove from the heat and keep warm.

! TAKE CARE !
The sauce scorches easily, so stir well.

3 PREPARE AND COOK THE KEBABS

1 About 30 minutes before cooking, soak the bamboo skewers (see box, right). Heat the broiler. Thread the chicken strips onto the skewers accordion-style, using 3 strips per skewer and slightly twisting the strips as you thread them.

Thread chicken strips onto skewers accordion-style

Hold skewer steady as you twist chicken strip slightly

To soak bamboo skewers
Put the skewers in a bowl, cover with cold water and let soak 30 minutes, then drain them.

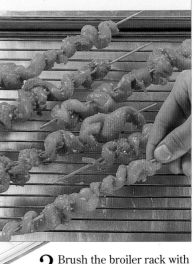

2 Brush the broiler rack with oil. Arrange the chicken kebabs on the rack.

3 Broil the kebabs 2-3 inches from the heat until the chicken is browned, 2-3 minutes. Turn and brown the other side, 2-3 minutes.

🍴 TO SERVE

Arrange the kebabs on individual plates and serve with the warm peanut sauce. Accompany with a rice pilaf for a more substantial meal.

Raw vegetable salad – shredded carrot and cabbage, sliced cucumber, and tomato dressed with mild vinegar – is excellent accompaniment for saté

VARIATION
VIETNAMESE CHICKEN KEBABS

1 Prepare the chicken breasts as directed, but cut them into ³/₄-inch cubes.

2 Make the marinade by mixing 3 shallots, finely chopped, 2 garlic cloves, finely chopped, 1 tsp seeded and finely chopped fresh green chili pepper, 2 tsp grated fresh ginger root, 3 tbsp soy sauce, and 2 tbsp each distilled white vinegar and vegetable oil.

3 Crush 1 stalk lemon grass with a rolling pin and add to the mixture.

4 Marinate the chicken cubes 3-12 hours, then thread onto 12 soaked bamboo skewers. Discard the lemon grass.

5 Broil the kebabs as before, and serve with the peanut sauce.

— GETTING AHEAD —

The peanut sauce can be made up to 2 weeks ahead and kept, covered, in the refrigerator. The chicken can be left to marinate 12 hours, but do not cook until just before serving.

CHICKEN IN RED WINE

Coq au Vin

 SERVES 4-6 ♨ WORK TIME 30 MINUTES* ☕ COOKING TIME 1½-1¾ HOURS

EQUIPMENT

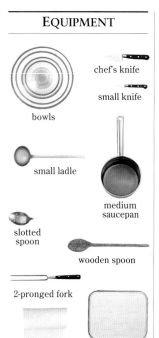

chef's knife

small knife

bowls

small ladle

medium saucepan

slotted spoon

wooden spoon

2-pronged fork

paper towels

plates

large flameproof casserole with lid

bowl strainer

plastic wrap

conical strainer

chopping board

ANNE SAYS
"This dish varies with the wine used – a Rhône wine gives a rich dark sauce, a Loire more fruity, and a Bordeaux more astringent."

In this classic Coq au Vin, the bird is marinated to tenderize and give it flavor, then simmered in a red wine sauce and served with a garnish of bacon dice, baby onions, and mushrooms. The more mature the chicken, the better the dish will be – French cooks use a boiling fowl or, best of all, the traditional male cock bird.

plus 12-18 hours marinating time

SHOPPING LIST

1	chicken, weighing 4-4½ lbs
¼-lb	piece of bacon
1 tbsp	vegetable oil
1 tbsp	butter
18-20	baby onions
½ lb	mushrooms
1	garlic clove
2	shallots
3 tbsp	flour
2 cups	chicken stock or water
1	bouquet garni
	salt and pepper
	For the marinade
1	onion
1	celery stalk
1	carrot
1	garlic clove
6	black peppercorns
1½ cups	red Burgundy wine
2 tbsp	olive oil

INGREDIENTS

carrot

butter

piece of bacon

chicken

mushrooms

onion

garlic cloves

red wine

celery stalk

baby onions

bouquet garni

shallots

olive oil

flour

black peppercorns

chicken stock

vegetable oil

ORDER OF WORK

1 CUT UP AND MARINATE THE CHICKEN

2 SAUTE THE CHICKEN

3 PREPARE THE GARNISH

4 FINISH THE COOKING

HOW TO CUT UP A CHICKEN INTO 8 PIECES

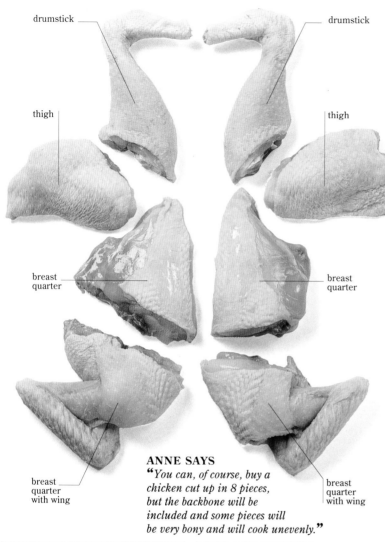

drumstick

drumstick

thigh

thigh

breast quarter

breast quarter

breast quarter with wing

breast quarter with wing

ANNE SAYS
"You can, of course, buy a chicken cut up in 8 pieces, but the backbone will be included and some pieces will be very bony and will cook unevenly."

1 Using a chef's knife, cut down between the leg joint and body on one side. Twist the bone sharply outward to break the joint, then cut through it and pull the leg from the body. Repeat this procedure for the other leg.

2 Slit closely along both sides of the breastbone to loosen the meat, then split the breastbone. Turn the bird over onto its breast and cut along one side of the backbone. The bird is now divided in half.

ANNE SAYS
"You can use poultry shears instead of a chef's knife, if you prefer; they are especially good for splitting the breastbone, cutting the backbone and rib bones, and cutting the breast and legs in half."

3 Cut the backbone and rib bones in one piece from the breast half where they are still attached, leaving the wing joints attached to the breast.

4 Cut each breast piece in half diagonally, cutting through the breast and rib bones so that a portion of the breast meat is cut off with the wing. Cut off any sharp bones.

5 Cut each leg in half through the joint, between the thigh and the drumstick, using the line of fat as a guide.

1 CUT UP AND MARINATE THE CHICKEN

1 To make the marinade, thinly slice the onion. Trim and thinly slice the celery. Thinly slice the carrot.

2 Put the onion, celery, carrot, garlic clove, and peppercorns in the saucepan, pour in the red wine, and bring to a boil. Simmer 5 minutes, then let cool completely.

3 Cut up the chicken into 8 pieces (see box, page 29). Put the chicken pieces in a bowl, pour on the cooled marinade, then spoon the olive oil on top. Cover with plastic wrap and marinate the chicken 12-18 hours in the refrigerator, turning the pieces occasionally.

Use bowl strainer with supports to free your hands for other chores

Marinating liquid and vegetables will be added separately

4 Remove the chicken pieces from the marinade and pat them dry with paper towels.

5 Strain the marinade through the bowl strainer and reserve both the liquid and the vegetables.

2 SAUTE THE CHICKEN

1 Cut the bacon into dice. Heat the oil and butter in the casserole until foaming, add the bacon, and fry until browned and the fat is extracted. Remove the bacon with the slotted spoon and reserve it.

2 Add the chicken pieces to the casserole, skin-side down, and cook until well browned, about 10 minutes.

3 Turn over the chicken pieces and brown the other side, then remove them.

Use long-pronged fork to protect your fingers from sizzling fat

HOW TO CLEAN AND QUARTER OR SLICE MUSHROOMS

1 Trim the stem from each mushroom just level with the cap. Wipe the mushrooms clean with damp paper towels. If they are dirty, swirl them in a bowl of cold water and lift out to drain in a colander.

2 **To quarter mushrooms:** Hold each mushroom on the chopping board stem-side down and cut into quarters.

To slice mushrooms: Hold each mushroom stem-side down and cut vertically into slices of the required thickness.

3 PREPARE THE GARNISH

1 Put the baby onions in a bowl, cover with hot water, and leave 2 minutes. Remove the onions and peel them.

Immerse onions in hot water to loosen skins

2 Clean the mushrooms and cut them into quarters (see box, page 31). Chop the garlic. Chop the shallots.

3 Add the baby onions to the casserole and sauté lightly until browned. Lift out with the slotted spoon and reserve. Add the mushrooms and sauté until tender, 2-3 minutes. Remove the mushrooms with the slotted spoon and reserve.

4 FINISH THE COOKING

1 Discard all but about 2 tbsp of the fat from the casserole and add the reserved vegetables from the marinade. Cook over very low heat until softened, 5 minutes. Sprinkle the flour over the vegetables and cook, stirring, until lightly browned, 2-3 minutes.

2 Stir in the reserved marinade and the chicken stock and add the chopped garlic and shallots, the bouquet garni, salt, and pepper. Heat to boiling, stirring well.

Use small ladle to press sauce through strainer

3 Replace the chicken pieces, cover, and simmer over low heat until the pieces are just tender when pierced with the 2-pronged fork, 45-60 minutes. Transfer the chicken pieces to a plate and keep warm; pour the sauce into a bowl.

4 Wipe the casserole and add the baby onions. Strain the sauce over them through the conical strainer, pressing down on the vegetables with the small ladle to extract the maximum flavor and liquid.

5 Simmer over low heat until the onions are almost tender, 5-10 minutes. Add the mushrooms and continue to simmer until the sauce is reduced and lightly coats the back of a spoon, 2-3 minutes longer. Taste for seasoning.

Sauce should adhere but not be too thick

6 Add the chicken pieces and bacon to the sauce and reheat gently 3-4 minutes.

🍽 **TO SERVE**

Spoon the chicken and sauce from the casserole onto warmed individual plates. Serve with steamed baby potatoes or potatoes fried in butter and oil.

V A R I A T I O N S

CHICKEN IN WHITE WINE
Coq au Vin Blanc

Prepare as for Chicken in Red Wine, but omit the bacon and replace the red wine in the marinade with an equal quantity of medium-dry white wine, such as a Riesling.

CHICKEN IN BEAUJOLAIS
Coq au Beaujolais
A lighter version of the classic Coq au Vin.

Prepare as for Chicken in Red Wine, but omit the bacon and mushrooms and replace the Burgundy red wine with an equal quantity of fruity red Beaujolais.

GETTING AHEAD

Chicken in Red Wine can be prepared up to 2 days ahead and kept, covered, in the refrigerator (the flavor will mature). Reheat it gently on the stove.

TEX-MEX CHICKEN SALAD

⦿| SERVES 4-6 ⟐ WORK TIME 20-25 MINUTES

EQUIPMENT

bowls

chopping board

small knife

chef's knife

boning knife

metal spoon

rubber gloves

whisk

forks

salad spinner

This salad is a meal in itself. Tortilla chips are the best accompaniment, but this dish goes equally well with a loaf of crusty French bread or whole wheat rolls.

GETTING AHEAD

The chicken can be roasted 2 or 3 days in advance and kept, well wrapped, in the refrigerator. The vinaigrette dressing can be prepared up to 1 week in advance and kept in a sealed jar or bottle at room temperature. Simply add the fresh tarragon just before serving.

INGREDIENTS

red bell pepper

whole cooked chicken

shallot

corn kernels

chili peppers

tomatoes

fresh tarragon

romaine lettuce

Dijon-style mustard

salad oil

red wine vinegar

SHOPPING LIST

1	whole cooked chicken, weighing 4 lbs, or 1 lb cooked skinless, boneless chicken
1-2	fresh chili peppers, to taste
2	large tomatoes
1	red bell pepper
1	shallot
1	large head of romaine lettuce, about 1 lb
³/₄ cup	drained canned corn kernels
	For the vinaigrette dressing
¹/₄ cup	red wine vinegar
2 tsp	Dijon-style mustard
¹/₂ tsp	salt
¹/₄ tsp	pepper
³/₄ cup	salad oil
3	sprigs of fresh tarragon

ORDER OF WORK

1 **PREPARE THE SALAD INGREDIENTS**

2 **ASSEMBLE THE SALAD**

ANNE SAYS
"If you don't have a salad spinner, pat the washed lettuce dry with paper towels or a clean dish towel."

1 PREPARE THE SALAD INGREDIENTS

1 If using a whole cooked chicken, remove the meat from the bones, discarding all skin and any gristle. With the chef's knife, cut the chicken meat into thin slices.

ANNE SAYS
"You should have about 3 cups of chicken meat in slices."

2 With the small knife, cut the stem from the chili pepper and halve the pepper lengthwise. Scrape out the seeds and inner white core.

! TAKE CARE !
When handling chilis, always wear rubber gloves to protect your hands from the alkaloid, capsaicin, which may irritate your skin.

3 Put one chili half on top of the other and slice thinly, then chop the slices into a fine dice.

Cut lettuce rolls across into strips

4 Core the tomatoes. With the chef's knife, cut the tomatoes crosswise into thin slices.

5 Core, seed, and dice the bell pepper (see box, below). Finely chop the shallot.

6 Pull the lettuce leaves from the core. Wash the leaves, then dry in the salad spinner. Stack 3 or 4 leaves and roll tightly. Slice into strips.

HOW TO CORE, SEED, AND DICE A BELL PEPPER

1 Cut around the pepper core, twist, and pull it out.

2 Halve the pepper. Cut away the protruding ribs and scrape out the seeds. Rinse the pepper under cold running water and pat dry.

3 Cut each pepper half lengthwise into thin strips, then cut the strips across into a fine dice.

HOW TO MAKE VINAIGRETTE DRESSING

1 Put the vinegar, mustard, salt, and pepper in a small bowl and whisk to combine them thoroughly and dissolve the salt.

2 Add the oil in a thin stream, whisking constantly so that the dressing emulsifies and thickens slightly.

3 Finely chop the tarragon. Stir the tarragon into the dressing and taste for seasoning.

ANNE SAYS
"Vinaigrette will last up to 1 week in a sealed jar or bottle. The dressing will separate but a brisk shake will re-emulsify the ingredients. Store at room temperature because some oils solidify when chilled. Add flavorings (shallots, herbs, or garlic) at the last minute so flavor is fresh."

2 ASSEMBLE THE SALAD

1 Make the vinaigrette dressing (see box, left). Combine the chicken and shallot in a large bowl. Add 3-4 tbsp of the dressing and toss well.

3 Arrange the lettuce on individual plates and mound the chicken on top. Arrange the tomatoes around the edges of the plates and spoon the corn on top of the tomatoes. Scatter the bell pepper on top of the chicken and drizzle with the remaining vinaigrette.

2 Put the lettuce in another large bowl. Add 3-4 tbsp of the vinaigrette dressing and toss.

4 With a fork, sprinkle lightly with the chili pepper and serve.

Tortilla chips are an excellent accompaniment for the salad, providing a crunchy contrast to the chicken and vegetables

Roquefort, or any blue cheese, adds sharp flavor

Bacon adds crisp texture

V A R I A T I O N

COBB SALAD

A California classic with a striking variety of colors.

1 Prepare the chicken, shallot, lettuce, tomatoes, and vinaigrette dressing as for Tex-Mex Chicken Salad (omitting the chili, red bell pepper, and corn).

2 Stack 6 slices of bacon (total weight about 6 oz) and cut crosswise into 1/2-inch strips. In a small frying pan, cook the bacon until browned. Drain on paper towels.

3 Crumble 3 oz roquefort or blue cheese.

4 Prepare and slice 2 avocados (see box, below).

5 Assemble the salad, sprinkling on lemon juice as necessary to prevent the avocados from discoloring, and serve.

HOW TO PREPARE AND SLICE AN AVOCADO

1 With a chef's knife, cut lengthwise around the avocado to the pit. Twist to loosen and separate the halves, then pull them apart.

2 Embed the blade of the knife in the pit and twist gently to remove. Alternatively, scoop out the pit with a spoon.

3 With a small knife, make a shallow incision in the skin of each avocado half, taking care not to cut into the flesh. Peel away the skin.

4 Cut the avocado halves lengthwise into thin slices. Lay the slices on a plate and sprinkle with lemon juice to prevent discoloring.

! TAKE CARE !
Use a stainless steel knife when slicing avocados to keep the flesh from discoloring.

SAUTE OF CHICKEN WITH PAPRIKA

 SERVES 4 WORK TIME 20-25 MINUTES COOKING TIME 40-50 MINUTES

EQUIPMENT

chef's knife   small knife

plastic bag

chopping board

small bowl

large sauté pan
with lid

2-pronged fork

wooden spoon

shallow dish

The basic sauté technique involves browning the chicken in fat, then cooking it in its own juices, with an addition of water, stock, or wine. Onion is almost always included among the flavorings, but there is no end to the variety of garnishes and sauces for sautéed chicken. This Hungarian-style version is just one example.

GETTING AHEAD

The sautéed chicken, and the sauce prepared through step 2, can be made up to 2 days ahead and kept, covered, in the refrigerator. Add the sour cream just before serving.

INGREDIENTS

chicken

red bell peppers   onion

butter

sour cream

vegetable oil

chicken
stock

tomato paste   paprika

SHOPPING LIST

1	chicken, weighing 3 - 3 1/2 lbs
3 tbsp	paprika
	salt and pepper
1	medium onion
1 tbsp	vegetable oil
1 tbsp	butter
1 cup	chicken stock
4	medium red bell peppers
1 tbsp	tomato paste
1/2 cup	sour cream

ORDER OF WORK

1 SAUTE THE CHICKEN

2 MAKE THE SAUCE

1 SAUTE THE CHICKEN

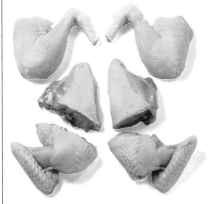

1 Cut up the chicken into 6 pieces (see Steps 1-4 of How to Cut Up a Chicken into 8 Pieces, page 29). Sprinkle the pieces with the paprika, salt, and pepper, patting to coat evenly. Chop the onion (see box, below).

2 Heat the oil and butter in the sauté pan over medium heat until foaming. Add the chicken legs, skin-side down, and sauté until they begin to brown, about 5 minutes. Add the breast pieces and continue cooking gently until very brown, about 10-15 minutes longer. Turn and brown the other side.

! TAKE CARE !
Do not let the paprika scorch or it will taste bitter.

3 Push the chicken to one side of the pan and add the onion to the other. Stir to combine with the fat, scraping the pan, and sauté until soft but not brown, about 3 minutes. Spread out the chicken again and add half of the stock. Cover and cook until the chicken is tender, 15-25 minutes. Meanwhile, roast, seed, and slice the bell peppers (see box, page 40).

4 To test for doneness, pierce the meat with the 2-pronged fork. The chicken is done when the juices run clear. If some pieces cook before others, remove them and keep warm.

HOW TO CHOP AN ONION

1 Peel the onion, leaving on the root to hold the onion together. Cut the onion in half and lay one half, cut-side down, on a chopping board. With a chef's knife, make a series of horizontal cuts from the stem toward the root. Cut just to the root of the onion but not through it.

2 Make a series of lengthwise vertical cuts, cutting just to the root but not through it.

ANNE SAYS
"When slicing, tuck your fingertips under and use your knuckles to guide the blade of the knife."

3 Slice the onion crosswise to dice it. (Adjust the distance between the slices depending on whether you want it coarse or fine. For finely chopped onion, continue chopping until you have the fineness required for the recipe.)

HOW TO ROAST, SEED, AND SLICE A BELL PEPPER

1 Roast the pepper under the broiler, turning as needed, until the skin is black and blistered, 10-12 minutes. Alternatively, hold the pepper with a 2-pronged fork over a gas flame until the skin is charred. Immediately put the pepper in a plastic bag, close it, and let cool (the steam trapped inside helps loosen the skin). Peel off the skin.

2 Cut around the pepper core and pull it out. Halve the pepper and scrape out the seeds with the knife. Rinse the pepper and pat dry.

3 With a chef's knife, cut each pepper half lengthwise into thin strips.

2 MAKE THE SAUCE

1 Remove all the chicken pieces from the pan and keep warm. Boil the pan juices, stirring, until reduced to a shiny glaze. Stir in the tomato paste. Add the remaining stock and stir until boiling.

Noodles, both plain and spinach, make a cool contrast to pungent paprika sauce

2 Return all the chicken pieces to the pan, add the bell pepper strips to the sauce, and heat through gently, 1-2 minutes.

3 Add most of the sour cream and shake the pan gently to mix it into the sauce. Taste for seasoning.

! TAKE CARE !
Do not boil the sauce after the sour cream has been added or it will curdle.

🍴 TO SERVE
Arrange the chicken pieces on individual plates; spoon the bell pepper strips and sauce on top, and then the remaining sour cream.

V A R I A T I O N
SAUTE OF CHICKEN WITH DARK BEER

The pungent flavors of beer and gin replace the spice in Sauté of Chicken with Paprika.

Flageolet beans, plainly boiled and tossed with butter and parsley, are a perfect accompaniment

Beer-based cream sauce contains hints of flambéed gin

1 Cut up the chicken as directed, then coat the pieces with 3-4 tbsp seasoned flour in place of the paprika.
2 Sauté the chicken, adding 2 chopped onions as directed. Add 3-4 tbsp gin to the sauté pan and heat, then light carefully with a match to flame it.
3 Add dark beer in place of the chicken stock, season with salt and pepper, and continue cooking as directed, skimming off any excess fat at the end of cooking.
4 Omit the red bell peppers and tomato paste, and finish the sauce with only 1/4 cup sour cream.
5 Chop a few sprigs of parsley and sprinkle over the chicken before serving.
6 Flageolet beans, lima beans, or fava beans, plainly boiled and tossed with a little butter and chopped parsley, are an excellent accompaniment for the chicken.

V A R I A T I O N
SZECHUAN PEPPER CHICKEN

A distant cousin of the classic Steak au Poivre, this uses aromatic Szechuan pepper rather than paprika to spice the chicken.

Wild rice is mixed with white to make an effective garnish

1 Toast 1/2 cup Szechuan pepper in a small dry pan over very low heat, tossing the pepper and shaking the pan until the pepper smells aromatic, 3-5 minutes.
2 Put the pepper in a plastic bag and crush finely with a rolling pin; alternatively, grind the pepper in a spice mill.
3 Cut up the chicken as directed, then coat the pieces with the pepper in place of the paprika.

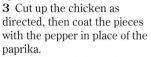

4 Sauté the chicken, adding the chopped onion and chicken stock as directed; omit the bell peppers.
5 To make the sauce, boil the pan juices to a shiny glaze. Add the remaining stock and boil again to a glaze; omit the tomato paste. Replace the sour cream with heavy cream; add it all to the pan juices, and boil, stirring, until the sauce is rich and slightly thickened, 1-2 minutes. Taste for seasoning.
6 Serve with mixed wild and white rice.

CHICKEN EN COCOTTE WITH LEMON AND PARMESAN

 SERVES 4   WORK TIME 15-20 MINUTES   COOKING TIME 45-55 MINUTES

EQUIPMENT

- large flameproof casserole with lid
- saucepan
- poultry shears
- small knife
- boning knife
- vegetable peeler
- spoon
- large metal spoon
- 2-pronged fork
- trussing needle and string
- whisk
- paper towels
- plate
- chopping board
- strainer
- aluminum foil
- small bowl

INGREDIENTS

chickens

lemons

butter

heavy cream

chicken stock

arrowroot *

Parmesan cheese

*potato starch can also be used

These young chickens are cooked in a covered pot to keep them moist, then halved to make attractive serving portions. The simple cream sauce, piquant with lemon and Parmesan cheese, is made from the pan juices. Serve with a selection of crisp-tender vegetables.

GETTING AHEAD

The chickens can be cooked and kept with their pan juices, covered, in the refrigerator up to 24 hours. Reheat the chickens 20-25 minutes in a 350°F oven, then make the sauce just before serving.

SHOPPING LIST

2	chickens, each weighing 2-2½ lbs
	salt and pepper
2	lemons
3 tbsp	butter
	For the cheese sauce
½ cup	chicken stock
½ cup	heavy cream
1 tsp	arrowroot or potato starch
1 tbsp	water
¼ cup	grated Parmesan cheese

ORDER OF WORK

1 COOK THE CHICKENS

2 MAKE THE CHEESE SAUCE

3 CUT THE CHICKENS IN HALF FOR SERVING

HOW TO TRUSS A CHICKEN

1 Wipe the inside of the chicken with paper towels and season it inside and out with salt and pepper.

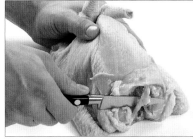

2 With a small knife, remove the wishbone.

3 Set the bird breast up and push the legs back and down. Insert a threaded trussing needle at the knee joint, and push it through the bird and out through the other knee joint.

Hold both feet steady with one hand

4 Turn the bird over so it is back-side up. Pull the neck skin over the neck cavity and tuck the wing tips over it. Push the needle through both sections of one wing and into the neck skin. Continue under the backbone of the bird to the other side. Push the needle through the second wing in the same way, through both wing bones.

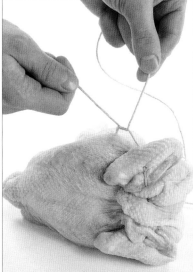

5 Turn the bird onto its side. Pull the ends of the string firmly together and tie them securely. Turn the bird breast up. Tuck the tail into the cavity of the bird and fold over the top skin. Push the needle through the skin.

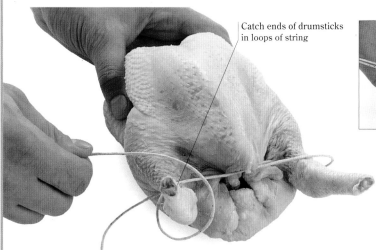

Catch ends of drumsticks in loops of string

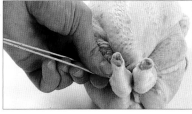

6 Loop the string around one drumstick, under the breastbone, and over the other drumstick. Tie the ends of the string together.

ANNE SAYS
"Chickens hold a better shape and are easier to carve if you truss them."

1 COOK THE CHICKENS

1 Heat the oven to 375°F. Truss the chickens (see box, page 43). Pare the zest from the lemons with the vegetable peeler.

2 Melt the butter in the casserole. Add one chicken and brown it on all sides, 5-10 minutes. Transfer it to the plate and brown the second chicken.

3 Return the first chicken to the casserole. Add the lemon zest and cover the casserole. Cook the chickens in the heated oven, turning them occasionally so they cook evenly.

ANNE SAYS
"Instead of pot roasting in the oven, the chickens can be cooked on top of the stove over low heat."

Scatter zest over both chickens

4 After 30-40 minutes, test the chickens for doneness by lifting them with the 2-pronged fork. The juices that run out should not be pink. Transfer the birds to the board, cover with foil, and keep them warm.

2 MAKE THE CHEESE SAUCE

Sit strainer securely in or on saucepan so you have both hands free to hold casserole

1 Remove the excess fat from the casserole and discard. Add the stock and bring to a boil, stirring to dissolve the pan juices.

2 Boil the stock until well reduced, about 5 minutes. Strain it into the saucepan.

3 Add the cream and whisk to mix, then bring just to a boil.

4 Stir the arrowroot or potato starch and water together in the small bowl to form a smooth paste. Whisk in enough of the paste to thicken the sauce: It should lightly coat the back of a spoon.

Whisk enough arrowroot or potato starch paste into sauce to thicken to desired consistency

5 Take the sauce from the heat and whisk in the Parmesan cheese. Taste for seasoning. Keep warm.

! TAKE CARE !
Do not reboil the sauce or the cheese may cook into strings.

3 CUT THE CHICKENS IN HALF FOR SERVING

Hold chicken securely
with 2-pronged fork

Poultry shears cut
through breastbone
more easily than
sharp knife

2 Cut along one side of the
breastbone with poultry shears.
Turn the bird over; cut along each
side of the backbone and discard it.
Repeat with the other bird.

1 Discard the trussing strings from
the chickens. Set a bird breast-side
up on the board. Slice closely along the
breastbone with the boning knife to
loosen the meat.

¶❍¶ TO SERVE

Set each chicken half on an
individual plate and spoon on the
sauce.

Crisp stir-fried vegetables
complement the lightly
sauced chicken
perfectly

Half a young chicken
makes an ideal serving for one,
giving both white and dark meat

Creamy sauce has rich tang of
Parmesan cheese

VARIATION
CHICKEN WITH THYME

Sprigs of fresh thyme delicately scent the chicken en cocotte here in place of the lemon zest.

1 Omit the lemon from the main recipe and instead cook the chicken with 4-5 sprigs of fresh thyme.
2 Make the cream sauce but do not add cheese.
3 Garnish the chicken with finely chopped fresh thyme, sprinkling it on in neat, curved lines if you like. Broccoli florets and fine sticks of zucchini make good accompaniments.

VARIATION
CHICKEN EN COCOTTE WITH JUNIPER BERRIES AND WILD MUSHROOMS

The earthy combination of juniper berries and wild mushrooms is ideal with chicken.

1 With a rolling pin, coarsely crush 2-3 tbsp juniper berries in a thick plastic bag.
2 Omit the lemon from the main recipe and instead add the juniper berries; cook as directed.
3 Trim the stems from 1/2 lb fresh wild mushrooms, such as shiitake or chanterelles, then clean them with damp paper towels. (Wild mushrooms are often covered with soil or twigs, so extra care must be taken with cleaning them; if they are very dirty, plunge them into a bowl of cold water, shake them to loosen the dirt, then drain in a colander.) Slice the caps vertically.
4 In a frying pan, sauté the mushrooms in 2 tbsp butter with salt and pepper until softened.
5 Make the cream sauce but do not add cheese; stir the sautéed mushrooms into the sauce after it has thickened.

BROILED CHICKEN THIGHS IN YOGURT

 SERVES 4   WORK TIME 20-25 MINUTES*   COOKING TIME 15-20 MINUTES

EQUIPMENT

paper towels

food processor**

plate

pastry brush

chef's knife

metal spatula

2-pronged fork

wooden spoon

chopping board

broiler pan and rack

large bowl

small saucepan

**blender can also be used

In this Middle Eastern-style recipe, plain yogurt plays a double role: First it tenderizes the chicken, then it helps thicken and enrich the sauce. During the summer months, stoke up your barbecue and grill the chicken outdoors. The chicken thighs and coriander sauce can be served hot or at room temperature.

GETTING AHEAD

The sauce can be prepared up to 24 hours ahead and kept, covered, in the refrigerator. Reheat it gently so that it does not boil and separate. The chicken can be marinated up to 24 hours, but broil it at the last minute.

* plus 3-4 hours marinating time

INGREDIENTS

garlic cloves

chicken thighs

onion

fresh coriander

plain yogurt

ground coriander

sour cream

vegetable oil

SHOPPING LIST

8	chicken thighs, total weight about 2½ lbs
1 cup	plain yogurt
	salt and pepper
	vegetable oil for broiler rack
	For the coriander sauce
1	medium onion
2	garlic cloves
2 tbsp	vegetable oil
2 tbsp	ground coriander
1 cup	plain yogurt
a few	sprigs of fresh coriander (cilantro)
½ cup	sour cream

ORDER OF WORK

1 PREPARE THE CHICKEN

2 COOK THE CHICKEN

3 MAKE THE CORIANDER SAUCE

PREPARE THE CHICKEN

1 Put the chicken thighs in the large bowl and pour the plain yogurt over the top. Season the yogurt with salt and pepper.

Stir yogurt to make it smooth before pouring

2 Turn the chicken thighs with your hands until the chicken is well coated with yogurt, then cover the bowl tightly, and set aside to marinate in the refrigerator 3-4 hours.

3 Heat the broiler. Brush the rack in the broiler pan with oil. Lift the chicken pieces out of the bowl and, with the metal spatula, scrape off the yogurt, discarding it.

Use metal spatula to spread coating evenly

4 Dry the chicken pieces with paper towels and arrange them on the oiled broiler rack.

HOW TO PEEL AND CHOP GARLIC

1 To separate the garlic cloves, crush the bulb with the palms of your hands, putting one on top of the other to exert pressure. Alternatively, pull a clove from the bulb with your fingers.

2 To peel the clove, lightly crush it with the flat of a chef's knife to loosen the skin. Peel off the skin with your fingers.

3 Set the flat side of the knife on top of the clove and strike firmly with your fist. Finely chop the garlic with the knife, rocking the blade back and forth.

2 COOK THE CHICKEN

1 Broil the chicken thighs, 3-4 inches from the heat, until the tops are very brown, about 8-10 minutes. Turn the pieces over.

2 Continue broiling until the pieces are very brown and no pink juice runs out when they are pierced with the 2-pronged fork, 7-10 minutes longer. While the chicken is cooking, make the sauce.

3 MAKE THE CORIANDER SAUCE

1 Chop the onion. Finely chop the garlic (see box, left). Heat the oil in the saucepan and sauté the onion until soft and starting to brown.

Ground coriander adds deliciously sweet and pungent taste

2 Add the ground coriander and garlic and continue cooking over low heat for 2-3 minutes, stirring constantly.

3 Purée the onion mixture with the yogurt in the food processor. Add the fresh coriander and purée just until it is chopped.

4 Return to the saucepan. Pour in the sour cream, then season with salt and pepper. Heat the sauce, stirring constantly. Taste for seasoning and keep warm.

! TAKE CARE !
When heating a sauce that contains sour cream or yogurt, do not let it boil or it will separate.

🍽 **TO SERVE**
Arrange 2 chicken thighs on each warmed plate and spoon the sauce around them.

Fresh mint sprigs add color to finished dish

Tabouleh salad is refreshing accompaniment to spicy chicken thighs

V A R I A T I O N

BROILED CHICKEN THIGHS WITH YOGURT AND HONEY

1 Marinate the chicken as for Broiled Chicken Thighs in Yogurt, adding 2 tbsp honey and 1 tsp ground ginger to the yogurt.
2 Meanwhile, spread ¼ cup pine nuts on a baking sheet and bake in a 375° F oven until evenly browned, 5-8 minutes; set aside.
3 Broil the chicken as directed, without scraping off the yogurt mixture and brushing with the excess yogurt mixture several times during broiling.
4 While the chicken is cooking, prepare the sauce as directed in the recipe for Broiled Chicken Thighs in Yogurt, omitting the ground and fresh coriander. After the sauce has been puréed, stir in the sour cream and ½ cup raisins and heat as directed.
5 Arrange the chicken on individual plates and sprinkle with the toasted pine nuts.
6 Serve the sauce separately or in lettuce cups as shown.
7 A green salad is a good accompaniment.

GROUND CHICKEN CUTLETS

Kuritsa Pojarski

🍽 SERVES 4   🥣 WORK TIME 35-40 MINUTES   🍲 COOKING TIME 40-50 MINUTES

EQUIPMENT

deep-fat fryer

deep-fat thermometer if needed

medium sauté pan

chef's knife

boning knife

small frying pan

baking sheet

slotted spoon

metal spatula

wooden spoon

chopping board

small ladle

pastry brush

metal skewer

shallow dishes

bowls

aluminum foil

meat grinder*

strainer

*food processor can also be used

This dish is a variation of traditional "pojarski," once a favorite of the Russian royal family.

GETTING AHEAD

The cutlets can be shaped through step 2 and refrigerated up to 12 hours. The sauce can be made and kept, covered, in the refrigerator up to 3 days.

SHOPPING LIST

6	individual brioches, total weight about 8 oz
½ cup	milk
14 oz	skinless, boneless chicken breast halves
3 tbsp	heavy cream
	ground nutmeg
	salt and pepper
¼ cup	seasoned flour
1	egg
	oil for deep frying
	For the tomato and mushroom sauce
1 lb	tomatoes
1	small onion
1	garlic clove
4 oz	mushrooms
2 tbsp	vegetable oil
1 tbsp	tomato paste
1	bouquet garni
	sugar

INGREDIENTS

chicken breast halves

brioches

bouquet garni

tomatoes

mushrooms

onion

garlic clove

seasoned flour

sugar

egg

milk

heavy cream

tomato paste

oil for deep frying

vegetable oil

ground nutmeg

ORDER OF WORK

1 **PREPARE THE CHICKEN MIXTURE**

2 **SHAPE AND COOK THE CUTLETS**

3 **MAKE THE TOMATO AND MUSHROOM SAUCE**

1 PREPARE THE CHICKEN MIXTURE

1 Cut 4 of the brioches into dice using the chef's knife, and set aside. Break apart the remaining brioches and put them in a small bowl.

Challah, egg bread, or sliced white bread can be substituted for brioche

2 Pour the milk over the brioches in the bowl and let soak 5 minutes. Squeeze any excess milk from the soaked brioches.

3 Remove the tendon from each chicken breast half (see box, below). Cut the chicken into chunks. Work it through the fine blade of the meat grinder with the soaked brioches.

HOW TO REMOVE THE TENDON FROM A CHICKEN BREAST HALF

Strip the tendon from the center of the breast half, stroking it with a boning knife to remove it cleanly. If the inner fillet becomes detached from the rest of the breast meat, replace it.

ANNE SAYS
"A food processor can also be used, but take care not to purée the meat too finely."

4 With the wooden spoon, beat the cream into the ground chicken mixture with a pinch of nutmeg and salt and pepper.

5 To test the mixture for seasoning, fry a little piece in the frying pan and taste – it should be well seasoned, so add more salt and pepper if required.

2 SHAPE AND COOK THE CUTLETS

1 With wet hands, shape the mixture into 4 balls and flatten slightly. Dip them in the seasoned flour and pat off the excess to obtain an even coating. Beat the egg and brush onto the rounds, draining off any excess.

2 Coat rounds in diced brioche, patting so they are completely covered. Chill uncovered in the refrigerator, about 30 minutes.

Fry cutlets in batches so they are not crowded in pan

3 Heat the oven to 375° F. Heat the oil for deep frying in the deep-fat fryer to 350° F. Add 1 or 2 cutlets to the hot oil and fry until brown all over, 2-3 minutes.

ANNE SAYS
"To test the oil temperature without a thermometer, drop in a cube of bread: It should turn golden brown in 1 minute."

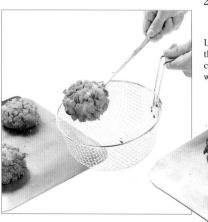

4 With the slotted spoon, transfer the cutlets to the baking sheet as they are fried. Fry the remaining cutlets in the same way.

Use skewer to check that cutlets are cooked all the way through

5 Bake the cutlets in the heated oven until the skewer inserted in the center is hot to the touch when withdrawn, 25-30 minutes. If the cutlets seem to be browning too quickly, cover them loosely with foil. While the cutlets are in the oven, make the sauce.

3 MAKE THE TOMATO AND MUSHROOM SAUCE

1 Chop the tomatoes. Chop the onion. Chop the garlic. Slice the mushrooms.

Press down well on tomato mixture

2 Heat half of the oil in the sauté pan, add the onion, and cook until browned, 2-3 minutes. Stir in the tomatoes, tomato paste, garlic, bouquet garni, salt, pepper, and a pinch of sugar, and cook, stirring occasionally, until fairly thick, 8-10 minutes.

3 Force the tomato mixture through the strainer into a bowl, using the small ladle and pressing down to extract all the pulp.

¶●¶ TO SERVE

Put each cutlet in the center of a warmed plate and spoon the sauce around it. Serve with an earthy accompaniment such as kasha (buckwheat grains).

4 Wipe the sauté pan, heat the remaining oil, and sauté the mushrooms until tender, without letting them brown. Stir in the tomato mixture and taste for seasoning.

Fresh herbs or salad leaves are an attractive garnish

VARIATION

COCKTAIL POJARSKI

These small golden, tasty balls are ideal finger food for parties. Garnish with salad leaves and black olives.

1 In the recipe for Ground Chicken Cutlets, cut the brioches into small dice and shape the pojarski mixture into 1-inch balls.

2 Proceed as directed; the pojarski will need only 5-10 minutes baking in the oven.

3 Serve on toothpicks without the sauce.

SAUTE OF CHICKEN WITH MUSSELS

 SERVES 4   WORK TIME 30-35 MINUTES COOKING TIME 40-50 MINUTES

EQUIPMENT

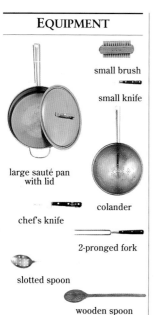

small brush

small knife

large sauté pan with lid

colander

chef's knife

2-pronged fork

slotted spoon

wooden spoon

large saucepan

shallow dish

chopping board

aluminum foil

Seasoned flour *is used for coating food to be sautéed or deep fried: Stir together ¼ cup all-purpose flour, 1 tsp salt, and ½ tsp pepper. This is enough to coat a 3- to 4-lb chicken, cut up into pieces.*

Combining mussels with chicken may sound unusual, but it's quite delicious, a distant cousin of paella. Juice from the steamed mussels adds an intense flavor to the dish. The orange meat of the mussels in their blue-black shells and the fresh green of chives and tender-crisp beans make for a colorful presentation.

GETTING AHEAD
The chicken pieces can be sautéed through step 4 and then refrigerated, covered, in the wine sauce up to 2 days. The green beans and mussels are best prepared just before finishing the dish. Reheat the chicken in the sauce, covered, about 10 minutes, then finish cooking the sauté.

SHOPPING LIST

1	chicken, weighing 3 - 3½ lbs
3-4 tbsp	seasoned flour (see box, left)
1 tbsp	vegetable oil
1 tbsp	butter
¼ cup	dry white wine
12 oz	green beans
18-24	mussels
½ cup	chicken stock
1	small bunch of fresh chives
	salt and pepper

INGREDIENTS

mussels

chicken

seasoned flour

butter

green beans

chicken stock

fresh chives

vegetable oil

white wine

ORDER OF WORK

1 SAUTE THE CHICKEN

2 COOK THE GREEN BEANS

3 CLEAN THE MUSSELS

4 FINISH COOKING THE SAUTE

SAUTE THE CHICKEN

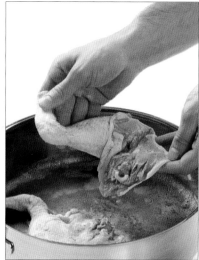

4 To test if the chicken is almost tender, pierce the meat with the 2-pronged fork: The chicken should fall easily from the fork. If some pieces cook before others, remove them and keep them warm.

1 Cut up the chicken into 6 pieces (see steps 1-4 of How to Cut Up a Chicken into 8 Pieces, page 29). Put the seasoned flour in the shallow dish. Dip the chicken pieces in the seasoned flour and pat off the excess with your hands to obtain an even coating.

2 Heat the oil and butter in the sauté pan over medium heat until foaming. Add the chicken legs, skin-side down, and sauté until they begin to brown, about 5 minutes. Add the breast pieces and continue cooking gently until very brown, about 10-15 minutes longer. Turn and brown the other side.

Low, straight sides allow steam to escape

3 Add the wine to the chicken. Cover and cook until the chicken is almost tender, 10-20 minutes. While the chicken is cooking, prepare the green beans and mussels (see page 58).

Wide heavy base of pan gives even heat

! TAKE CARE !
Use a long-handled, 2-pronged fork like this to protect your hands from intense heat and steam.

2 COOK THE GREEN BEANS

1 With your fingers, snap the ends off the beans. Put the beans in the colander and rinse them under cold running water.

2 Bring a large saucepan of salted water to a boil. Add the beans and cook until just tender, 5-8 minutes for medium beans; tiny beans may take as little as 3-4 minutes, large beans up to 12 minutes.

3 Drain the beans in the colander, rinse them under cold running water to stop the cooking, then leave them to drain again thoroughly.

3 CLEAN THE MUSSELS

1 Scrub the mussels under cold running water with the small brush, discarding any with broken shells or that do not close when tapped. Using the small knife, scrape off the barnacles from the shells. Detach and discard any weeds or "beards" from the mussels.

ANNE SAYS
"To clean barnacles quickly from mussels, rub 2 shells together."

Mussel shells should
be tightly closed

Detach stringy
"beards" – mussels
use these to cling to
poles or ropes where
they grow

! TAKE CARE !
While cleaning mussels, discard any with cracked or broken shells or that do not close after washing. After cooking, discard any that have not opened.

4 FINISH COOKING THE SAUTE

1 Set the mussels on top of all the chicken pieces in the sauté pan, cover, and cook until the mussels open, about 5 minutes.

2 With the slotted spoon and 2-pronged fork, transfer the mussels and chicken to a baking dish. Cover with foil and keep warm in a low oven. Add the chicken stock to the pan and boil until the sauce is reduced and slightly syrupy, 3-5 minutes, stirring occasionally.

Remove chicken and mussels from sauté pan while you finish sauce

3 Chop the chives. Return the chicken, mussels, and green beans to the sauté pan with the chopped chives and heat gently 2-3 minutes. Taste for seasoning.

V A R I A T I O N

CHICKEN WITH CLAMS

In this variation, hard-shell clams are combined with chicken. Choose small, tender clams.

1 Replace the mussels with the same amount of hard-shell clams, cleaning and cooking the clams in exactly the same way as the mussels.
2 As a light decoration, top each portion of chicken with 2-3 crossed chive stems.
3 Plainly cooked rice is a good foil for the intense flavors in this dish.

¶❍¶ TO SERVE
Put the chicken pieces on individual plates with the mussels and green beans. Spoon the sauce over and around.

Steamed mussels are delicious with chicken

PINWHEEL CHICKEN WITH HERBS AND GOAT CHEESE

🍽 SERVES 4 ⌣ WORK TIME 30-40 MINUTES ♨ COOKING TIME 15-20 MINUTES

EQUIPMENT

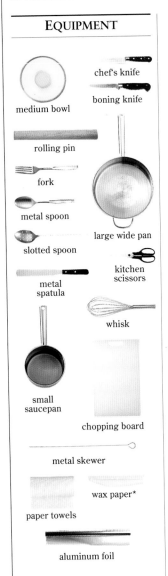

- medium bowl
- chef's knife
- boning knife
- rolling pin
- fork
- metal spoon
- slotted spoon
- large wide pan
- metal spatula
- kitchen scissors
- whisk
- small saucepan
- chopping board
- metal skewer
- wax paper*
- paper towels
- aluminum foil

*plastic wrap can also be used

This dish uses flattened chicken breasts, rolled with an herb-and-goat-cheese stuffing, then poached. When sliced, the pretty green filling makes a spiral pattern, hence the name pinwheel. A simple, steamed vegetable, such as tiny zucchini, balances the tomato butter sauce.

GETTING AHEAD
The chicken rolls can be cooked, drained, and kept in their foil in the refrigerator up to 24 hours. Reheat them in a pan of simmering water for 7-10 minutes – be careful not to overcook them or they will be tough.

SHOPPING LIST

4	large skinless, boneless chicken breast halves, total weight about 1¹/₂ lbs
1	small bunch of fresh basil
1	small bunch of parsley
3	sprigs of fresh thyme
4 oz	goat cheese
2-3 tbsp	light cream, if necessary
	juice of ¹/₂ lemon
	salt and pepper
	For the tomato butter sauce
3	shallots
1 cup	dry white wine
¹/₂ cup	butter
1 tbsp	tomato paste

INGREDIENTS

- goat cheese
- chicken breast halves
- fresh thyme
- fresh basil
- white wine
- tomato paste
- shallots
- light cream
- butter
- parsley
- lemon juice

ORDER OF WORK

1 PREPARE THE CHICKEN BREASTS

2 STUFF THE BREASTS

3 COOK THE CHICKEN ROLLS

4 MAKE THE TOMATO BUTTER SAUCE

5 FINISH THE DISH

1 PREPARE THE CHICKEN BREASTS

3 Pound the split-open breasts lightly with the rolling pin to obtain flat steaks of even thickness.

ANNE SAYS
"You can also use a meat pounder for flattening the chicken breasts."

Cover with paper to keep rolling pin from sticking

1 Remove the tendon from each chicken breast half: Stroke out the tendon with the boning knife to remove it cleanly. Separate the fillet from the breast by lifting the end of the fillet and pulling it toward you. Set the fillets aside.

2 With the chef's knife, split the breast open by slicing three-quarters of the way through the meat, holding it firmly with the flat of your hand, so the long straight edge of the breast forms the hinge. Open the split breast, like a book, and place it between 2 sheets of moistened wax paper or plastic wrap. Repeat this process for the remaining breasts.

2 STUFF THE BREASTS

2 Put the goat cheese in the bowl and mash with the fork (harder cheese may be crumbled by hand), discarding any rind. If the cheese is too dry, soften it with the cream.

1 Chop the basil, parsley, and thyme with the chef's knife.

Add cream to cheese if it is dry

3 Add the herbs and lemon juice to the cheese and mix thoroughly. Taste for seasoning.

ANNE SAYS
"Fresh goat cheese will be soft enough to mash without added liquid, but more mature cheese will have a drier, more crumbly texture and will need cream to soften it so that it can be spread."

4 Peel the top sheet of wax paper from each breast. With the metal spatula, evenly spread one-quarter of the herb-and-goat-cheese filling in the center of each flattened breast.

Spread goat-cheese-and-herb filling in even layer over flattened chicken breast

Leave border of chicken breast clear all around so that filling will not be squeezed out when breast is rolled up

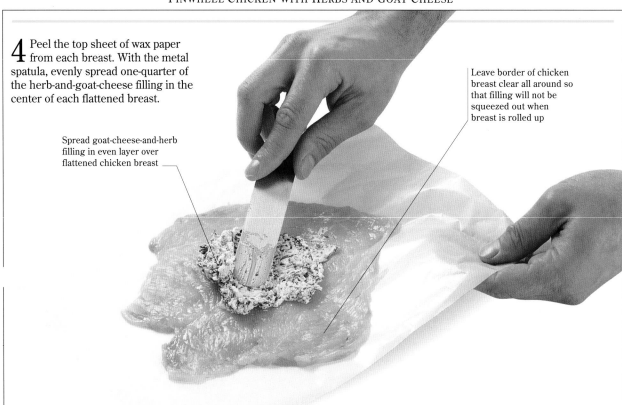

5 Put the fillet on top of the filling, along one long edge of a breast. Loosen the breast from the paper.

6 Roll up the chicken breast into a neat cylinder, beginning with the fillet-topped end.

7 Fold in the ends of the roll so the filling is securely sealed in. Repeat with the remaining breasts.

3 COOK THE CHICKEN ROLLS

1 Cut a piece of foil to wrap generously around a rolled breast and put it on the work surface, shiny-side down. Set the breast on the foil.

2 Roll up the stuffed breast in the foil neatly and tightly, smoothing the foil to keep it taut.

3 Twist the ends of the foil firmly to form a tight cylinder, sealing in the ends. Repeat the process for the remaining rolled breasts.

4 Half fill the wide pan with water and bring to a boil. With the slotted spoon, put the foil packages in the water and simmer until the skewer inserted in the center of a package is hot to the touch when withdrawn, about 15 minutes. Keep the chicken rolls warm in their foil packages in the pan of hot (not boiling) water while you make the sauce.

Replace packages in hot water to keep warm

4 MAKE THE TOMATO BUTTER SAUCE

2 Off the heat, whisk in the butter, a small piece at a time, whisking constantly and moving the pan on and off the heat. Do not boil; the butter should thicken the sauce creamily without melting to oil.

1 Finely chop the shallots. In the small saucepan, boil the shallots, wine, and a small pinch each of salt and pepper until reduced to a syrupy glaze.

Add butter one piece at a time; and wait until melted and absorbed before adding next piece

3 Whisk in the tomato paste and taste for seasoning.

! TAKE CARE !

Butter sauces are delicate, and separate easily if overheated. To keep them warm, set the saucepan in another pan of warm, not hot, water. Whisk occasionally but never leave more than 30 minutes.

5 FINISH THE DISH

Sharp knife cuts cleanly through chicken and filling without squashing

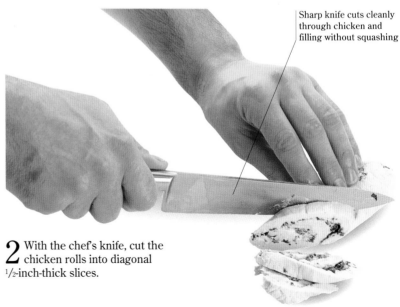

1 Remove the chicken rolls from the pan with the slotted spoon and carefully unwrap them on paper towels to absorb any water.

2 With the chef's knife, cut the chicken rolls into diagonal ¹/₂-inch-thick slices.

3 Spoon the sauce onto warmed individual plates, arrange the pinwheel slices on top, and serve.

V A R I A T I O N

PINWHEEL CHICKEN ITALIENNE

In this recipe, flattened chicken breasts are rolled with Parma ham and nutty-flavored fontina cheese.

1 Prepare the chicken breast halves as directed in the main recipe for Pinwheel Chicken.

2 Trim 4 large pieces, or 8 smaller pieces, of thinly sliced Parma ham the same size as the flattened breasts. Set the ham on the chicken.

3 Cut a 4-oz piece of fontina cheese into thin slices, discarding the rind. Lay the cheese along one long side of each breast and put the fillet on top.

4 Roll up, wrap, and poach the breasts as directed.

5 Prepare the butter sauce, omitting the tomato paste.

6 For an attractive presentation, strain the sauce to separate the shallots, then garnish with the shallots and steamed, finely diced, zucchini.

Fan-cut zucchini are simple to prepare but look very elegant

Cherry tomatoes and mint sprig add color to presentation

ORIENTAL STIR-FRIED CHICKEN

🍽 SERVES 4　🥣 WORK TIME 15-20 MINUTES*　🍲 COOKING TIME 10-12 MINUTES

EQUIPMENT

wok with stirrer**

baking sheet

chef's knife

boning knife

spoon

strainer　　paper towels

bowls

chopping board

**large heavy frying pan can also be used

ANNE SAYS

"*After you have finished cooking, do not wash your wok; just wipe it with a damp cloth or paper towels while it's still warm.*"

Stir-frying invites endless variations – the key is to use fresh ingredients, finely cut to ensure quick, even cooking. Here chicken is lightly marinated and united with celery, Chinese mushrooms, and almonds.

GETTING AHEAD

The vegetables and chicken can be prepared up to 1 hour ahead, and the almonds toasted a day in advance.

* plus 25-30 minutes marinating and soaking time

INGREDIENTS

chicken breast halves

dried Chinese　broccoli
black mushrooms

celery stalks

onion

sliced　vegetable　sesame
almonds　oil　oil

rice wine　soy sauce

cornstarch

SHOPPING LIST

1 oz	dried Chinese black mushrooms
1 cup	warm water, more if needed
½ cup	sliced almonds
1	medium onion
4	celery stalks
1	medium head of broccoli, about 1 lb
2	skinless, boneless chicken breast halves, total weight about ¾ lb
6 tbsp	vegetable oil
1 tsp	sesame oil
	For the marinade
¼ cup	soy sauce
¼ cup	rice wine or dry sherry
2 tsp	cornstarch

ORDER OF WORK

1. **PREPARE THE VEGETABLES AND ALMONDS**

2. **SLICE AND MARINATE THE CHICKEN**

3. **COOK THE STIR-FRY**

1 PREPARE THE VEGETABLES AND ALMONDS

1 Put the mushrooms in a bowl, cover with the warm water, and let soak 30 minutes.

ANNE SAYS
"If you cannot find dried Chinese mushrooms, ½ lb fresh mushrooms, cleaned and sliced, can be substituted."

2 While the mushrooms are soaking, toast the almonds and prepare the remaining vegetables. Heat the oven to 375°F. Spread the almonds evenly on the baking sheet and toast in the oven until lightly browned, 6-8 minutes.

3 Cut the onion lengthwise in half. Cut each half into 4 or 5 wedges.

4 Trim the ends from the celery stalks and cut the stalks crosswise, on the bias, into ½-inch-thick slices.

5 Cut off the broccoli heads, discarding the stems. Cut the heads into very small florets.

6 Drain the mushrooms, reserving the liquid. Trim off any hard, woody stems, then slice the mushrooms. Strain the liquid through the strainer lined with paper towels to remove any grit or sand.

2 SLICE AND MARINATE THE CHICKEN

1 Remove the tendon from each chicken breast half. Separate the fillet from each breast half by lifting the end of the fillet and pulling it toward you. With the chef's knife, cut the fillet into thin strips.

2 Holding your hand firmly on top of the breast, cut the meat on the bias into very thin slices. You should get 10-15 slices from each breast.

3 In a bowl, mix together the soy sauce, rice wine, and cornstarch, stirring until the cornstarch is dissolved. Add the chicken and stir until coated. Marinate about 15 minutes while you cook the vegetables.

3 COOK THE STIR-FRY

1 Heat half of the vegetable oil in the wok. Add the onion and celery and stir and toss over quite high heat until the vegetables begin to soften, 1-2 minutes.

2 Add the broccoli and fry, stirring and tossing constantly, until it begins to soften, 2-3 minutes. Stir the mushrooms into the vegetables and cook, stirring and tossing, about 2 minutes.

! TAKE CARE !
If using fresh mushrooms, be sure to cook them until all liquid has evaporated.

3 Remove all the vegetables from the wok to a bowl and set them aside in a warm place.

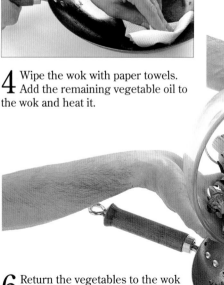

4 Wipe the wok with paper towels. Add the remaining vegetable oil to the wok and heat it.

Tip warm vegetables back into wok

5 Drain the chicken slices and strips, reserving the marinade liquid. Add the chicken to the wok and cook over high heat, stirring and tossing, until the chicken is no longer opaque, 2-3 minutes.

6 Return the vegetables to the wok and stir to mix with the chicken. Add ¼ cup of the reserved mushroom soaking liquid.

7 Pour in the reserved marinade liquid and cook, stirring, 2 minutes. As the marinade liquid cooks, the cornstarch will slightly thicken the sauce. Sprinkle the stir-fry with the sesame oil, stir, and taste for seasoning, adding more soy sauce, rice wine, or sesame oil to your taste.

8 Sprinkle the toasted almonds over the stir-fry and serve in individual bowls.

Chicken slices are delicately flavored with rice wine and soy sauce

Chopsticks accent Asian roots of this dish

V A R I A T I O N

SWEET AND SOUR STIR-FRIED CHICKEN

Here pineapple replaces the broccoli and mushrooms and pineapple juice gives sweetness to the sauce.

1 Prepare the chicken breasts as directed in the main recipe.
2 For the marinade, reduce the rice wine to 1 tbsp; add 1 tbsp wine vinegar and 1 tbsp sugar.
3 Omit the broccoli and mushrooms and replace with 4 rings of canned pineapple cut into small pieces.
4 Finish as directed, adding ¼ cup pineapple juice from the can instead of the mushroom soaking liquid.

YORKSHIRE CHICKEN WITH STUFFED PRUNES

Hindle Wakes

🍴 SERVES 4   🥣 WORK TIME 30 MINUTES*   🍲 COOKING TIME 1¼-1½ HOURS

EQUIPMENT

 chef's knife

 food processor

shallow dishes

chopping board

trussing needle and string

2-pronged fork   wooden spoon

 grater

medium baking dish

 saucepans

 large metal spoon

citrus juicer

 whisk

 kitchen string

bowls

 flameproof casserole or pot with lid

 strainer

Tradition has it that Hindle Wakes was created to reward those who kept watch or "wake" on the eve of a great festival.

* plus 1 hour soaking time

SHOPPING LIST

1	stewing chicken, weighing 4 lbs, with liver
2	medium carrots
1	bouquet garni (see box, page 72)
2	cloves
1	medium onion
2	garlic cloves
1 tsp	black peppercorns
1¼ cups	medium dry white wine
1½ quarts	chicken stock or water, more if needed
	salt and pepper
	For the stuffing
½ lb	large pitted prunes
1	small onion
½ cup	butter + extra for baking dish
1	bunch of parsley
1	lemon
10	slices of white bread, total weight about ½ lb
½ cup	chicken stock
	For the velouté sauce
⅓ cup	butter
⅓ cup	flour
¾ cup	heavy cream
	lemon juice

INGREDIENTS

  garlic cloves

 stewing chicken

onion   prunes   lemon

 parsley

slices of white bread

 carrots   cloves

 black peppercorns

heavy cream   chicken stock

    bouquet garni   butter

white wine   flour

ORDER OF WORK

1. **PREPARE THE STUFFING**

2. **TRUSS AND POACH THE CHICKEN**

3. **COOK THE PRUNES AND STUFFING**

4. **MAKE THE VELOUTÉ SAUCE**

1 PREPARE THE STUFFING

1 Put the prunes in a bowl and cover with hot water. Let them soak until softened and plump, about 1 hour, then drain. Set aside 8-12 of the firmest prunes to be stuffed; chop the rest.

Reserve firmest, whole prunes for stuffing

Chop remaining prunes coarsely

2 Finely chop the onion. Heat half of the butter in a small saucepan, add the onion, and fry until soft but not brown, 2-3 minutes.

3 Cut any membrane from the chicken liver, then chop it.

4 Stir the chicken liver into the onion and cook until brown, 1-2 minutes. Turn into a bowl.

! TAKE CARE !
When grating lemon, be careful not to catch the white pith because it is bitter.

5 With the chef's knife, finely chop the parsley.

6 Grate the zest from the lemon, then cut the lemon in half and squeeze the juice.

Use juicer that will catch lemon seeds

7 Break up the bread and work it in the food processor or a blender to make crumbs. Melt the remaining butter in a small saucepan.

8 Add the chopped prunes, bread crumbs, parsley, and lemon zest to the bowl. Stir in the chicken stock, lemon juice, and melted butter. Season well to taste with salt and pepper. Set aside.

Stir stuffing ingredients to combine thoroughly

HOW TO MAKE A BOUQUET GARNI

This package of aromatic flavoring herbs is designed to be easily lifted from the pot and discarded at the end of cooking. To make, hold 2-3 sprigs of thyme, 1 bay leaf, and 10-12 parsley stems together. Wind a piece of string around the herbs and tie securely, leaving a length of string to tie to the pot handle.

2 TRUSS AND POACH THE CHICKEN

1 Truss the chicken. Put the chicken into the casserole (it should just fit). Cut the carrots into quarters and add to the casserole. Add the bouquet garni, tying the string to the handle so that it can be removed easily at the end of cooking.

2 Stick the cloves into the onion and add to the casserole, along with the garlic and peppercorns.

4 Bring to a boil, skimming well, then cover and simmer over low heat, skimming occasionally, 1¼ - 1½ hours.

3 Add the white wine with enough chicken stock or water to cover the chicken above the legs. Season lightly with salt.

Skim off scum and impurities from time to time during simmering

5 Halfway through cooking, turn the chicken over so that it cooks evenly. (At this point, cook the prunes and stuffing; see page 74.) The chicken is done when the thigh meat is tender and no pink juice runs out when it is pierced with the 2-pronged fork.

Use 2-pronged fork and spoon or ladle to turn chicken over gently so that cooking liquid does not splash out of casserole

6 When the chicken is cooked, remove it from the casserole, wrap it in foil, and keep warm; reserve the cooking liquid for the sauce.

3 COOK THE PRUNES AND STUFFING

Add about 1 teaspoonful of filling

1 Heat the oven to 375° F. Fill the whole prunes with stuffing, mounding it. Butter the baking dish and spread the remaining stuffing in it.

2 Arrange the stuffed prunes on top of the stuffing and cover the dish with foil. Bake until very hot, 30-40 minutes. Take out and keep warm.

4 MAKE THE VELOUTE SAUCE

1 Skim any fat from the cooking liquid and discard. Boil the cooking liquid until reduced by half.

2 Strain the cooking liquid and measure it: There should be about 3 cups. Add more stock or water if necessary. Discard the vegetables and bouquet garni.

Pour liquid through strainer set in bowl

3 Melt the butter in a medium saucepan. Whisk in the flour.

Whisk constantly as you add strained liquid

4 Cook the mixture until foaming but not browned, 1-2 minutes, whisking well.

5 Add the cooking liquid and heat, whisking constantly, until the sauce comes to a boil and thickens. Add the cream and simmer 2 minutes. Take from the heat, stir in lemon juice and seasoning to taste, and keep warm.

🍽 **TO SERVE** Cut the stuffing into wedges. Remove the trussing strings from the chicken, carve it, arrange on warmed plates, and coat with sauce. Place the prunes and stuffing next to the chicken. Serve the rest of the sauce separately.

—— **GETTING AHEAD** ——
Chicken, prunes, and stuffing can be prepared a day ahead. Refrigerate chicken in cooking liquid; reheat and make sauce just before serving.

CHICKEN IN PARSLEY SAUCE

1 Remove the stems from a bunch of parsley and lightly bruise or crush them with a rolling pin to release all the flavor; chop the sprigs.
2 Poach the chicken as directed in the main recipe, adding the parsley stems to the cooking liquid.
3 Omit the stuffing and prunes.
4 Prepare the sauce as directed, and add the chopped parsley with the lemon juice.

ANNE SAYS
"*To preserve the bright green color of chopped parsley, blanch it before adding it to the sauce: Sprinkle the parsley into a small saucepan of boiling water, simmer 5 seconds, and drain in a fine strainer. Rinse the parsley under cold water and spread to dry on paper towels.*"

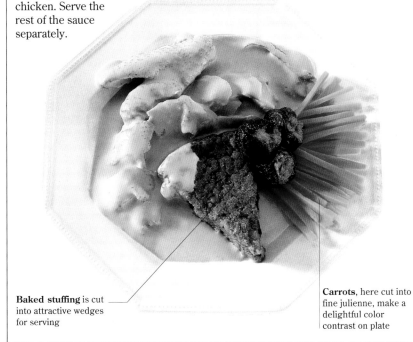

Baked stuffing is cut into attractive wedges for serving

Carrots, here cut into fine julienne, make a delightful color contrast on plate

BRUNSWICK STEW

 SERVES 4-6 WORK TIME 25-35 MINUTES COOKING TIME 2-2½ HOURS

EQUIPMENT

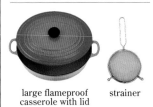

large flameproof casserole with lid

strainer

small knife

chef's knife

large metal spoon

2-pronged fork

slotted spoon

bowls

chopping board

forks

wooden spoon

saucepans, 1 with lid

kitchen string

shallow dish

ANNE SAYS

"If you don't have a ham hock, use a piece of smoked slab bacon. Before serving, cut it into dice, discarding any rind."

Brunswick County in North Carolina and in Virginia both take credit for this famous colonial American stew. Two things are certain: The recipe uses Southern ingredients – smoked ham, lima beans, corn, and an enlivening kick of hot pepper – and it was originally made with squirrel and without vegetables!

GETTING AHEAD

The stew can be cooked 2 days ahead and kept refrigerated; in fact, the flavor mellows on standing. Brunswick Stew also freezes well.

SHOPPING LIST

1	chicken, weighing 3-3½ lbs
1	smoked ham hock, weighing about 1 lb
1½ quarts	water, more if needed
1 tbsp	dark brown sugar
1	bouquet garni
1	medium onion
3	celery stalks
3	medium tomatoes, total weight about ¾ lb
1¾ cups	shelled fresh or thawed frozen lima beans
1½ cups	fresh or thawed frozen corn kernels
2	large potatoes, total weight about ¾ lb
1 tsp	dried hot red pepper flakes
	salt and pepper

INGREDIENTS

chicken

onion   smoked ham hock

corn kernels   tomatoes

bouquet garni   potatoes

dark brown sugar   lima beans   dried hot red pepper flakes

celery stalks

ORDER OF WORK

1 COOK THE CHICKEN

2 PREPARE AND COOK THE VEGETABLES

3 COOK THE POTATOES AND FINISH THE STEW

COOK THE CHICKEN

1 Cut up the chicken into 6 pieces (see steps 1-4 of How to Cut Up a Chicken into 8 Pieces, page 29). Put the chicken pieces in the casserole with the ham hock and pour in enough water to cover. Add the sugar and bouquet garni. Bring to a boil and skim well with the slotted spoon.

2 Cover and simmer gently until the chicken pieces are almost tender when pierced with the 2-pronged fork, about 1 hour.

3 Lift out the chicken with the slotted spoon and reserve it. Remove the casserole from the heat and set aside.

HOW TO PEEL, SEED, AND CHOP TOMATOES

1 With a small knife, cut the core out of each tomato, then turn the tomato over and mark a cross on the base. Immerse the tomatoes in a pan of boiling water 8-15 seconds, depending on ripeness, until the skin curls away from the cross.

3 When the tomatoes are cool, drain them and peel away the skin, using the small knife.

5 Set each tomato half cut-side down on a chopping board and slice it with a chef's knife. Turn the slices through 90° and slice them again.

2 With a slotted spoon, lift the tomatoes out of the water and transfer them to a bowl of cold water.

Squeeze out seeds into strainer so that juices can be reserved

4 Halve each tomato crosswise like a grapefruit. Squeeze each half firmly in your fist to remove the seeds, scraping off any remaining seeds with the knife.

6 Coarsely chop the tomatoes into rough dice.

2 PREPARE AND COOK THE VEGETABLES

Drain thawed frozen corn before adding

1 Chop the onion. Trim and thinly slice the celery. Peel, seed, and coarsely chop the tomatoes (see box, page 77).

2 Bring the chicken liquid in the casserole back to a boil. Add the onion, celery, tomatoes, and lima beans to the chicken liquid and simmer, stirring often, until the beans are nearly tender, 20-30 minutes.

3 Add the corn and simmer 10 minutes longer. While the vegetables are simmering, cook the potatoes (see below).

3 COOK THE POTATOES AND FINISH THE STEW

1 Cut the potatoes into equal chunks and put them in a saucepan of salted water. Bring the water to a boil, then cover and simmer until the potatoes are tender when pierced with the point of the small knife, 15-20 minutes. Drain the potatoes in the strainer, then work them through the strainer with the wooden spoon.

ANNE SAYS
"You can crush the potatoes with a potato masher if you prefer. Just drain off the water using the saucepan lid and crush the potatoes in the saucepan."

Press potatoes through strainer to purée finely

2 Stir the potatoes and red pepper flakes into the stew and season to taste. Return the chicken pieces to the stew and simmer, stirring often, until the chicken is very tender, about 15 minutes longer.

ANNE SAYS
"You can also use a food mill for puréeing the potatoes."

! TAKE CARE !
Do not use a food processor or electric mixer because this will give the potatoes a gluey consistency.

3 Lift out the ham hock. Using a fork and knife, pull the meat from the bones, discarding the skin and fat.

4 Shred the meat with 2 forks and stir it back into the stew. The sauce should be thick, but if it is sticky, add a little more water. Discard the bouquet garni and taste for seasoning.

⊗ TO SERVE
Serve the stew from the casserole or in individual bowls.

CHICKEN STEW BASQUAISE

1 Double the amount of tomatoes in Brunswick Stew, and omit the brown sugar, lima beans, and corn kernels.
2 Roast, peel, and core 2 red bell peppers and 2 green bell peppers and cut them into strips.
3 Add the peppers to the stew with the tomatoes.

CHICKEN WITH KIDNEY BEANS AND KIELBASA

Replacing the lima beans and corn with red beans and kielbasa (or any other garlic sausage for poaching) gives color and spice to the stew.

1 Soak 1 lb dried red kidney beans in plenty of cold water (to cover by about 3-4 inches) 6-8 hours; drain.
2 Put the beans in a pot and add 1 onion stuck with a clove and a bouquet garni. Cover generously with water and bring to a boil. Boil at least 5 minutes, then simmer 30 minutes; add salt and simmer about 45 minutes longer.
3 Drain the beans, discarding the onion and bouquet garni.
4 Cut a ³/₄-lb piece of kielbasa into thick slices, discarding the skin.
5 Prepare and cook the chicken as directed in the main recipe. Omit the lima beans and corn kernels. Add the kidney beans with the onion, tomatoes, and celery and simmer until the beans are nearly tender, about 30 minutes.
6 Thicken the stew with the potatoes, and add the kielbasa when you return the chicken to the stew.

Chicken and vegetables are a meal in themselves, needing only crusty bread as an accompaniment

CHICKEN IN A PAPER CASE WITH JULIENNE VEGETABLES

Suprêmes de Poulet en Papillote à la Julienne

🍴 SERVES 4   🥄 WORK TIME 30-40 MINUTES   🍲 COOKING TIME 10-15 MINUTES

EQUIPMENT

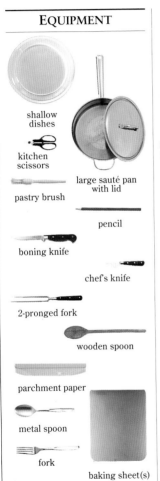

shallow dishes

kitchen scissors

pastry brush

large sauté pan with lid

pencil

boning knife

chef's knife

2-pronged fork

wooden spoon

parchment paper

metal spoon

fork

baking sheet(s)

chopping board

small bowl

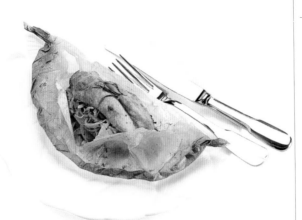

These puffed, golden-brown paper cases should be broken open at the table, so the full aromas of the chicken, herbs, and vegetables sealed inside can be appreciated by each diner. Take advantage of the seasons, altering the herbs and vegetables to follow your inspiration – tender asparagus spears with chives or chervil in the spring or wild mushrooms with rosemary in the fall.

— GETTING AHEAD —
The chicken breasts can be prepared and sealed in their paper cases up to 2 hours ahead and refrigerated. Bake them just before serving.

SHOPPING LIST

4	skinless, boneless chicken breast halves, total weight about 1½ lbs
¼ cup	seasoned flour
1 tbsp	vegetable oil
5-6 tbsp	butter
1	bunch of fresh tarragon
2	medium carrots
3	celery stalks
1	medium turnip
	salt and pepper
1	egg for glaze

INGREDIENTS

chicken breast halves

egg

seasoned flour

vegetable oil

turnip

butter

fresh tarragon

celery stalks

carrots

ORDER OF WORK

1 PREPARE THE CHICKEN BREASTS

2 PREPARE THE VEGETABLES

3 COOK THE VEGETABLES

4 MAKE THE PAPER CASES AND BAKE

PREPARE THE CHICKEN BREASTS

1 With the boning knife, gently stroke the tendon from each chicken breast half to remove it cleanly.

Chicken breasts should have even coating of seasoned flour

2 Separate the fillet from each breast by lifting an end of the fillet and pulling it toward you. With the chef's knife, cut the fillet into thin strips on the diagonal.

3 Put the seasoned flour in a shallow dish. Dip the chicken breasts in the flour and pat off the excess to obtain an even coating.

4 Heat the oil and 1 tbsp of the butter in the sauté pan until foaming. Sauté the breasts over brisk heat until browned, 1-2 minutes. Turn the breasts and brown on the other side.

ANNE SAYS
"If the pan is small, sauté the breasts in 2 batches."

5 Transfer the breasts to a shallow dish and allow to cool. (The meat will not be cooked through at this point; cooking is finished in the oven.)

6 Add the strips of fillet meat to the pan and sauté over medium heat, stirring, until they are no longer opaque, about 1 minute. Remove and let them cool. Wipe the sauté pan.

7 When the breasts are cool enough to handle, cut a pocket in each, holding them flat with your hand.

2 PREPARE THE VEGETABLES

1 Reserve 4 sprigs of tarragon for garnish. Remove the leaves from the remaining tarragon sprigs and chop them.

Julienne vegetables cook quickly and look very decorative

Cut vegetables into fine matchstick-sized strips

2 With the chef's knife, cut the carrots, celery stalks, and turnip into julienne strips (see box, right).

HOW TO CUT JULIENNE VEGETABLES

1 For round vegetables such as carrots, cut a thin strip from one side so that the vegetable will lie flat on the board.

2 Cut the vegetable crosswise into 2-inch lengths, then lengthwise into thin vertical slices.

3 Stack the slices, 6 or so at a time, and cut lengthwise into very fine strips, guiding the knife with your curled fingers. Use a strip as a guide for length when cutting other vegetables.

3 COOK THE VEGETABLES

1 First make a paper lid to fit the sauté pan: Fold a square of parchment paper in half and then in half again to make a triangle.

2 Fold the triangle of paper over once or twice more to form a slender cone.

4 Warm 3-4 tbsp of the remaining butter until soft and brush a little over the paper round. Heat the remaining 1 tbsp butter in the sauté pan. Add the vegetable julienne with salt and pepper to taste.

Position tip of cone over center of pan

Cut to size so paper will fit neatly inside pan

3 Holding the paper cone over the pan with the tip at the center, use the edge of the pan as a gauge to cut the cone. Unfold the paper round.

Cover vegetables with buttered paper and then with lid so they cook gently in their own juices

5 Set the paper round on the vegetables, butter-side down. Cover the pan with the lid and cook over low heat, stirring occasionally, until the vegetables are tender, 15-20 minutes.

! TAKE CARE !
Do not let the vegetables brown.

MAKE THE PAPER CASES AND BAKE

1 Fold a large sheet (about 15 x 18 inches) of parchment paper in half. Put one chicken breast on the paper and draw a curve to make a heart shape when unfolded. It should be at least 3 inches larger all around than the chicken breast. Cut along the curve to make a heart shape, cutting inside the drawn line. Repeat to make a total of 4 paper hearts.

Draw heart shape on folded paper

ANNE SAYS
"Foil is a practical alternative to parchment paper for the packages, but the presentation is less impressive because foil does not puff and brown."

2 Open out the paper hearts and brush each one with softened butter, leaving a border of about 1 inch unbuttered.

3 For the glaze, use the fork to beat the egg with ½ tsp salt. Brush the egg glaze on the unbuttered border of each paper heart.

Fold paper over chicken and vegetables so edges meet neatly

4 Heat the oven to 350°F. Stir the strips of chicken fillet into the vegetables and then add the chopped tarragon. Mix well and taste for seasoning.

5 Spoon a bed of the julienne filling on one half of a paper heart. Spoon more filling into the pocket of one of the chicken breasts and set it on the bed of vegetables. Lay a sprig of tarragon on top of the breast.

6 Fold the paper over the breast and run your finger along the edge to stick the 2 sides of the paper heart together.

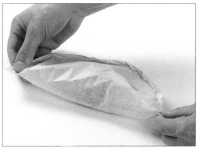

7 Make small pleats to seal the edges of the paper case.

8 Twist the "tails" of the paper case to finish. Repeat the process with the remaining ingredients to make 4 paper packages.

9 Lay the paper cases on the baking sheet(s) and bake them in the heated oven until puffed and brown, 10-12 minutes.

🍽 TO SERVE

At once, transfer the puffed, brown papillotes to warmed individual plates and serve. Each person can open his or her own chicken-filled paper case.

Chicken is moist and tender cooked this way

V A R I A T I O N

CHICKEN IN A PAPER CASE WITH BELL PEPPERS

Suprêmes de Poulet en Papillote Basquaise

1 Replace the carrots, celery, and turnip with 1 green bell pepper, 1 red bell pepper, and 1 yellow bell pepper.
2 Core and seed the peppers, then cut them into thin strips. Cook them as for the carrots, celery, and turnip.
3 Prepare the chicken breasts, fill the paper cases (omitting the tarragon), and bake as directed.

ANNE SAYS
"If the paper packages cool and deflate, they can be puffed again by warming briefly in the oven."

CHICKEN WITH CURRY DRESSING AND SAFFRON RICE

Salade de Poulet Indienne

🍽 SERVES 4-6   🥣 WORK TIME 25-35 MINUTES   🍲 COOKING TIME 20-30 MINUTES

EQUIPMENT

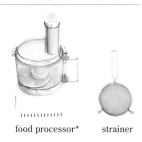

food processor*   strainer

small knife

chef's knife

rubber spatula

saucepans, 1 with lid

wooden spoon

forks

metal spoons

bowls

chopping board

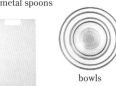

whisk   shallow dish

*blender can also be used

The dressing used here is unusual, lightly thickened with cottage cheese and flavored with curry and chutney. Saffron rice provides a brilliant background to the cold roast chicken.

GETTING AHEAD

The curry dressing, saffron rice, tomatoes and vinaigrette dressing can be prepared up to 24 hours ahead.

SHOPPING LIST

1	whole cooked chicken, weighing 4 lbs
3 tbsp	lemon juice
³/₄ cup	salad oil
1 lb	cherry tomatoes
1-2 tsp	paprika for sprinkling
	For the curry dressing
1	small onion
6 tbsp	salad oil
1 tbsp	curry powder
¹/₄ cup	tomato juice
¹/₄ cup	red wine vinegar
2 tsp	apricot jam
2 tbsp	lemon juice
1 cup	cottage cheese
	salt and pepper
	For the saffron rice salad
	saffron
2¹/₂ cups	water
1¹/₂ cups	long-grain rice
3	celery stalks

INGREDIENTS

cherry tomatoes   onion

apricot jam

whole cooked chicken

saffron

lemon juice

cottage cheese

celery

tomato juice

paprika

long-grain rice

curry powder

salad oil   red wine vinegar

ORDER OF WORK

1. MAKE THE SAFFRON RICE

2. MAKE THE CURRY DRESSING

3. PREPARE THE CHICKEN

4. FINISH THE RICE AND PREPARE THE CHERRY TOMATOES

1 MAKE THE SAFFRON RICE

1 Put a large pinch of saffron and a pinch of salt in a large saucepan with the water. Bring to a boil and simmer 2 minutes. Stir the rice into the saffron water and bring back to a boil. Cover and simmer until the rice is tender, 15-20 minutes. Let the rice cool 5-10 minutes, then stir with a fork and taste for seasoning. Set aside.

! TAKE CARE !
Do not stir the rice while it is very hot or the grains will break up.

Only a little saffron is needed to flavor and color rice

2 MAKE THE CURRY DRESSING

1 Finely chop the onion. Heat 1 tbsp oil in a small saucepan over medium heat. Add the chopped onion and sauté until soft but not brown, stirring occasionally.

2 Add the curry powder and cook gently 2 minutes, stirring. Add the tomato juice and vinegar and simmer until reduced by half.

! TAKE CARE !
Use a metal spoon for stirring the mixture because a wooden spoon will absorb strong flavors.

Pour in oil slowly, with machine running, so it is absorbed and dressing is emulsified

3 Stir in the apricot jam. Let the mixture cool, then transfer to the food processor.

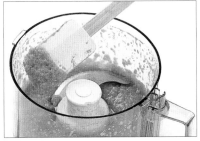

4 Blend until the mixture is smooth, scraping the bowl with the spatula as necessary.

5 Add the lemon juice and cottage cheese and blend until smooth. With the blades turning, pour in the remaining oil. Taste for seasoning.

3 PREPARE THE CHICKEN

Grasp rib cage with one hand and meaty part of thigh with other to remove leg

1 Using the chef's knife, cut down between the leg and body joints. Twist the leg sharply outward to break the joint, then cut through it and pull the leg from the body. Repeat the procedure for the other leg.

2 Slit along one side of the chicken breastbone. Using your fingers and the point of the knife, loosen the breast meat from the carcass, removing the breast half in one piece. Repeat for the other breast half.

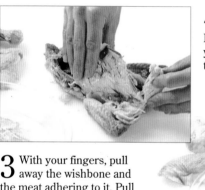

4 Pull off the skin from the chicken breast pieces and discard it. Pull the meat into shreds with your fingers and pile on the dish.

3 With your fingers, pull away the wishbone and the meat adhering to it. Pull off any remaining meat from the chicken carcass.

Pull skin up and off

5 Using your fingers and the point of the knife, tear and cut the meat from the leg bones. Trim away the tendons and discard the skin. Shred the meat with your fingers and add to the plate.

ANNE SAYS
"There should be about 3 cups of meat."

4 FINISH THE RICE AND PREPARE THE CHERRY TOMATOES

2 Make a vinaigrette dressing: Put the lemon juice, salt and pepper in a small bowl and whisk to combine. Add the oil in a thin stream, whisking constantly so that the dressing thickens slightly. Pour three-quarters of the dressing onto the rice and toss gently with 2 forks to combine. Reserve the remaining dressing.

ANNE SAYS
"Vinaigrette dressing can be kept for a week or more, in a tightly closed jar or bottle. It will separate, but a brisk shake will re-emulsify it."

1 Trim and thinly slice the celery. Stir gently into the cooled saffron rice with a fork. Transfer the mixture to a bowl.

3 Put the tomatoes, in 2 batches, in the strainer and immerse them in a medium saucepan of boiling water 8-10 seconds. Drain the tomatoes and strip off the skin with the small knife. Mix them with the reserved vinaigrette dressing.

Tomatoes are easy to peel after blanching in boiling water

🍽 **TO SERVE**

Toss the shredded chicken with half of the curry dressing. Pile the saffron rice salad in the center of a platter and arrange the chicken on top. Sprinkle with the paprika and garnish with the cherry tomatoes. Serve the remaining dressing separately.

Dressing for chicken is smooth and spicy

V A R I A T I O N

CHICKEN WITH TARRAGON DRESSING AND RICE

Chicken and tarragon are a natural pair.

1 Prepare the chicken and the cherry tomatoes as in the main recipe, cutting the chicken into slices.
2 Prepare the rice salad as directed but omit the saffron.
3 Replace the curry dressing with this dressing: Purée 1 cup cottage cheese in a food processor or blender with 1 tbsp tarragon vinegar. Chop 1 bunch of fresh tarragon and stir it into the puréed cottage cheese. Season to taste with salt and pepper.
4 Arrange on individual plates and garnish with a few sprigs of fresh tarragon.

SOUTHERN FRIED CHICKEN WITH PAN GRAVY

  SERVES 4   WORK TIME 10-15 MINUTES*   COOKING TIME 20-30 MINUTES

EQUIPMENT

chopping board

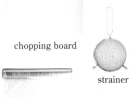

strainer

plastic wrap

shallow dish

large bowl

whisk

chef's knife

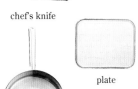

plate

paper towels

large heavy skillet

slotted spoon

large metal spoon

2-pronged fork

deep-fat thermometer

INGREDIENTS

chicken

milk

vegetable oil

flour

This is an American favorite from the South. In this version, the chicken is soaked in milk to whiten the meat. The traditional accompaniment is mashed potatoes, which can be accented with a sprinkling of chopped fresh herbs such as parsley or chives. Fried chicken, without the gravy, is also delicious served cold on a picnic, with a potato salad and some crisp vegetable sticks.

GETTING AHEAD

The chicken can soak up to 24 hours. If serving hot, do not fry in advance or the coating will be soggy.

* plus 8-12 hours soaking time

SHOPPING LIST

1	chicken, weighing 3-3½ lbs
2 cups	milk, more if needed
1 cup	vegetable oil for frying, more if needed
½ cup	seasoned flour, made with 2 tsp pepper
	For the gravy
2 tbsp	flour
1½ cups	milk
	salt and pepper

ORDER OF WORK

1 PREPARE THE CHICKEN

2 MAKE THE GRAVY

1 PREPARE THE CHICKEN

Cube of bread will sizzle when oil is sufficiently hot

3 Pour enough vegetable oil into the skillet or a frying pan to make a ³/₄-inch-deep layer. Heat the oil over moderate heat to 350°F on the deep-fat thermometer.

ANNE SAYS
"If you don't have a deep-fat thermometer, test the temperature of the oil by dropping a cube of fresh bread into it: If the bread turns golden brown in 1 minute, the oil is at about 350°F."

1 Cut up the chicken into 8 pieces (see box, page 29). Put the chicken pieces in the bowl and add enough milk to cover. Cover securely with plastic wrap and soak 8-12 hours.

Flour chicken pieces lightly

4 Put the seasoned flour in the shallow dish. Dip the chicken pieces in the flour and pat off the excess with your hands to obtain an even coating.

2 With the slotted spoon, transfer the chicken to the plate. Discard the milk.

ANNE SAYS
"To coat the chicken quickly, drop the pieces into a plastic bag, add the seasoned flour, twist the bag closed, and shake about 30 seconds."

5 Gently add the chicken pieces to the skillet, skin-side down, taking care because the chicken may sputter. Fry until brown, 3-5 minutes.

6 Turn the chicken pieces over and reduce the heat to low.

7 Continue frying until the chicken is brown and tender when pierced with the 2-pronged fork, 20-25 minutes. If some pieces cook before others, remove them and keep warm.

8 Transfer the chicken pieces to the plate lined with paper towels and keep warm.

! TAKE CARE !
If keeping the chicken warm in a low oven, do not cover it or the crisp coating will soften.

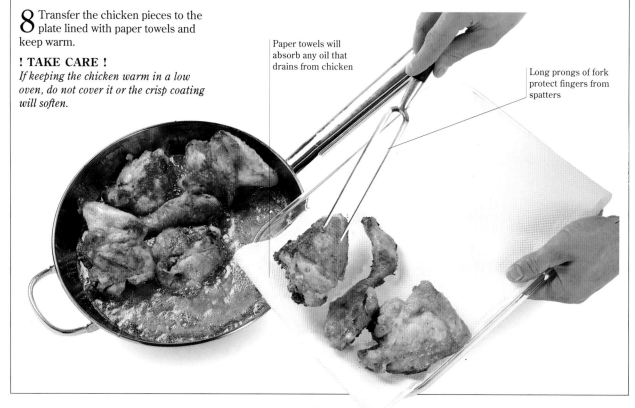

Paper towels will absorb any oil that drains from chicken

Long prongs of fork protect fingers from spatters

2 MAKE THE GRAVY

1 Discard all but about 2 tbsp of the fat from the skillet. Sprinkle in the flour.

2 Cook, stirring with the large metal spoon, until browned, 2-3 minutes.

3 Whisk in the milk and simmer the gravy until thickened, about 2 minutes. Season to taste and strain into a gravy boat.

¶❍¶ TO SERVE
Arrange the chicken pieces on a serving dish or individual plates. Serve the gravy separately.

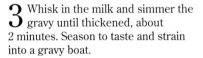

V A R I A T I O N
BACON-FRIED CHICKEN

In this recipe, the chicken does not cook in as deep a layer of fat as in Southern Fried Chicken, but the flavor of the bacon is wonderful and the gravy is spiked with a little Tabasco.

1 Soak the chicken in milk as directed in the main recipe.
2 Omit the vegetable oil and fry 8-12 slices of bacon until crisp and brown. Remove the bacon, drain on paper towels, and keep warm.
3 Flour the chicken as directed, then cook in the bacon fat, and drain on paper towels.
4 Prepare the pan gravy, adding a dash of Tabasco when seasoning.
5 Crumble the bacon slices and sprinkle over the chicken pieces when serving.

Fried chicken pieces are delicious hot or cold

STUFFED BABY CHICKENS WITH GRAPES

Coquelets en Cocotte Véronique

 SERVES 4   WORK TIME 35-45 MINUTES   COOKING TIME 1¼-1½ HOURS

EQUIPMENT

large flameproof casserole with lid

medium saucepan

kitchen scissors

fork

knife

metal spoons

bowls

paper towels

kitchen string

plate

slotted spoon

whisk

2-pronged fork

metal skewer

aluminum foil

strainer   baking sheet

In this recipe small birds are stuffed and tied, then roasted "en cocotte" in a covered pot. Any small birds such as squab or Cornish hens can be substituted for baby chickens. The stuffing is made from a pilaf of couscous, while "véronique" is a classic French garnish of cream and grapes.

INGREDIENTS

baby chickens

butter   chicken stock

slivered almonds   arrowroot   couscous

heavy cream   grapes

vegetable oil   port wine

SHOPPING LIST

4	baby chickens, weighing about 1 lb each
2 tbsp	butter
1 tbsp	vegetable oil, more if needed
	salt and pepper
	For the stuffing
½ cup	slivered almonds
1 cup	boiling water
1¼ cups	quick-cooking couscous
2 tbsp	butter
	For the sauce
½ cup	red port wine
1½ cups	seedless red or green grapes, removed from stem
1 cup	chicken stock
2 tsp	arrowroot or potato starch
2 tbsp	water
¼ cup	heavy cream

ORDER OF WORK

1. MAKE THE STUFFING

2. STUFF AND TIE UP THE CHICKENS

3. COOK THE CHICKENS

4. MAKE THE SAUCE

1 MAKE THE STUFFING

1 Heat the oven to 350°F. Spread the almonds on the baking sheet and toast in the heated oven until browned, 10-12 minutes. Remove the almonds and increase the oven heat to 375°F.

2 Pour the boiling water over the couscous and let stand to absorb the water, 2 minutes. Alternatively, cook the couscous according to package directions.

3 Dice the butter with the knife. Add the diced butter and toasted almonds to the couscous while still hot, and stir with the fork to remove any lumps. Season the stuffing to taste.

2 STUFF AND TIE UP THE CHICKENS

1 Wipe the birds inside and out with paper towels. Fill each baby chicken with the stuffing, packing it loosely. Pull the flap of skin over the stuffing to enclose it.

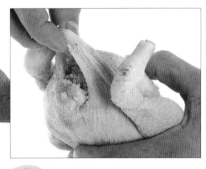

Pack stuffing lightly because it swells during cooking

! TAKE CARE !
The birds must be cooked immediately after stuffing because the meat can spoil quickly.

2 Tuck the neck skin and wings under the bird, then pass the string under the tail and tie a knot over the leg joints.

3 Bring the strings along the sides of the body and loop them around the legs. Tie them tightly.

4 Bring the strings under the bird and tie them under the body.

5 Tuck the wing bones behind the back and tie securely.

3 COOK THE CHICKENS

1 Melt the butter with the oil in the casserole over medium high heat. Put 2 of the baby chickens in the pot, breast down, and brown them on all sides, 5-10 minutes. Season with salt and pepper and remove. Repeat the process with the remaining 2 birds, adding more oil if necessary.

2 Replace the birds in the casserole, cover, and cook in the heated oven until they are very tender, 50-60 minutes. Test by pricking the thickest part of a thigh with the skewer; the juice should run clear, not pink. Also insert the skewer into the stuffing; it should be hot to the touch when withdrawn. With the slotted spoon, transfer the chickens to the plate. Cover them with foil and keep warm.

Tight-fitting lid keeps chicken juices from evaporating

ANNE SAYS
"The birds will cook more quickly if they are left empty and the stuffing is baked, covered, in a separate dish. Allow 30-40 minutes for the chickens, 10-15 minutes for the stuffing."

4 MAKE THE SAUCE

Grapes are flavored with port

1 In the saucepan, boil the port over high heat until reduced by half. Add the grapes and simmer 1 minute. Lift out the grapes using the slotted spoon and set aside.

2 Discard any fat from the casserole. Add the stock and boil over high heat, stirring to dissolve the pan juices, until reduced by half.

3 Strain the juices into the reduced port. Heat them until boiling, stirring well.

4 Stir the arrowroot or potato starch and water together to form a smooth paste. Whisk the paste into the port mixture. It will thicken at once to form a sauce.

5 Stir the cream into the sauce, then add the grapes and bring back to just boiling. Taste for seasoning.

🍽 **TO SERVE** Remove the strings. Set the chickens on individual plates. Spoon some sauce and grapes on the plates. Serve the remaining sauce and grapes separately.

Green beans or broccoli are good accompaniments

Couscous stuffing is scooped out onto plate

VARIATION

STUFFED BABY CHICKENS WITH CHILI SAUCE

To complement the couscous stuffing you can make a sauce with Middle Eastern flavorings.

1 Stuff and cook the birds as for Stuffed Baby Chickens with Grapes but serve with the following sauce:

2 Peel, seed, and chop 1 lb tomatoes. Chop 1 onion and sauté it in 1 tbsp vegetable oil until soft. Add the tomatoes, 3 tbsp chicken stock, 1/2 tsp ground coriander, and 1 tsp harissa (Moroccan chili sauce) or cayenne to taste. Cook until reduced and thick, 10-20 minutes. Add 1/3 cup pitted, chopped black olives. Taste for seasoning.

3 Discard any fat from the pan after cooking the chickens. Dissolve the pan juices in 1/2 cup chicken stock and add to the tomato sauce.

—— GETTING AHEAD ——

The baby chickens and sauce can be prepared, through step 3 of making the sauce, up to 24 hours ahead. Pour the reduced port and stock over the cooked baby chickens, cover tightly, and keep refrigerated. Before finishing the sauce, reheat the chickens in a 350° F oven, 20-25 minutes.

CHICKEN MOUSSE WITH MADEIRA BUTTER SAUCE

 SERVES 4   WORK TIME 25-35 MINUTES* COOKING TIME 20-30 MINUTES

EQUIPMENT

meat grinder

small frying pan

kitchen scissors

bowls

boning knife

pastry brush

pencil

wooden spoons

saucepans

colander

flameproof baking dish

parchment paper

6 medium ramekins (6 fl oz each)

chef's knife

metal spoon

metal spatula

slotted spatula

shallow dishes

whisk

chopping board

metal skewer

This chicken dish – a smooth, creamy mousse wrapped in fine slices of zucchini – makes an excellent hot first course, or it can be served as a light main course if saffron rice (see page 87) is added as an accompaniment.

GETTING AHEAD

The chicken mousse can be made 1 day ahead and refrigerated. Reheat in a water bath on top of the stove 10-15 minutes. The sauce should be made shortly before serving. It can be kept warm up to 30 minutes by placing the saucepan in a water bath containing warm water, but it will separate if it gets too hot.

* plus 15-30 minutes chilling time

SHOPPING LIST

1 lb	skinless, boneless chicken breast halves
2	egg whites
	salt and pepper
	ground nutmeg
3/4 cup	heavy cream
2	medium zucchini
	butter for ramekins
	For the Madeira butter sauce
2	garlic cloves
2	shallots
1/2 cup	butter
3 tbsp	Madeira
1 tbsp	heavy cream

INGREDIENTS

chicken breast halves

butter

garlic cloves

shallots

heavy cream

ground nutmeg

egg whites

Madeira

zucchini

ORDER OF WORK

1. MAKE THE CHICKEN MOUSSE MIXTURE

2. PREPARE THE ZUCCHINI

3. PREPARE THE RAMEKINS

4. ASSEMBLE AND COOK THE CHICKEN MOUSSE

5. MAKE THE SAUCE AND FINISH THE DISH

1 MAKE THE CHICKEN MOUSSE MIXTURE

1 Remove the tendon from each chicken breast half. With the chef's knife, cut the chicken into chunks. Work it through the fine blade of the meat grinder. Transfer the ground chicken to a medium bowl and set it in a larger bowl of ice water.

ANNE SAYS
"A meat grinder gives the mousse a light texture. A food processor can be used if you prefer, but take care not to purée too finely."

Keep mixture cold over ice water while beating in cream

2 Whisk the egg whites until frothy. With a flat wooden spoon, gradually add the egg whites to the chicken, beating the mixture until smooth and firm after each addition. Season with salt, pepper, and a pinch of nutmeg. If the mixture is soft, chill to stiffen it.

ANNE SAYS
"A damp cloth underneath the bowl of ice water holds it steady as you beat."

3 Beat in the cream, a little at a time. Chill the mixture over the bowl of ice water or in the refrigerator, 15 minutes, or until firm. The mixture should be stiff enough to hold its shape. To test the mixture for seasoning, fry a little piece in the frying pan and taste. Adjust seasoning if necessary.

2 PREPARE THE ZUCCHINI

Slice zucchini neatly

1 Trim the zucchini and cut into very thin slices. Bring a saucepan of salted water to a boil. Add the zucchini and simmer until softened, 1-2 minutes.

2 Drain the zucchini slices in the colander, rinse under cold water to stop the cooking, then drain thoroughly on paper towels.

3 PREPARE THE RAMEKINS

Parchment paper keeps mousse from sticking to bottom of ramekin

1 Using the base of a ramekin as a guide, draw 6 circles on a sheet of parchment paper. Cut out the paper circles just inside the pencil line.

2 Butter the ramekins. Lay a paper circle in the bottom of each ramekin; brush the paper with butter. Heat the oven to 350° F.

4 ASSEMBLE AND COOK THE CHICKEN MOUSSE

1 Line the bottoms and sides of the ramekins with overlapping slices of zucchini.

Mousse should reach top of zucchini

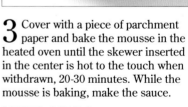

3 Cover with a piece of parchment paper and bake the mousse in the heated oven until the skewer inserted in the center is hot to the touch when withdrawn, 20-30 minutes. While the mousse is baking, make the sauce.

! TAKE CARE !
During baking, do not let the water boil or the mousse will separate.

2 Spoon the chicken mousse mixture into the ramekins, smoothing the top. Put the ramekins in the baking dish. Pour in boiling water to come more than halfway up the sides of the ramekins. Bring the water to a boil on top of the stove.

5 MAKE THE SAUCE AND FINISH THE DISH

1 Finely chop the garlic. Finely chop the shallots. Heat about 2 tbsp of the butter in a small saucepan, add the garlic and shallots, and cook, stirring, 2-3 minutes. Add the Madeira and boil, stirring to dissolve the pan juices, until reduced to a syrupy glaze, 2-3 minutes.

2 Add the cream and boil again until reduced to a glaze. Take the pan from the heat and add the remaining butter, a few pieces at a time, whisking constantly and moving the pan on and off the heat.

! TAKE CARE !
The butter should thicken the sauce creamily without melting to oil. If the sauce gets too hot, it will separate.

Set plate upside-down on ramekin to unmold mousse

🍴 TO SERVE
Using the slotted spatula and a dish towel, drain excess liquid from the side of each ramekin, then unmold each mousse onto a warm plate and spoon the sauce around.

Hold ramekin in dish towel

VARIATION

COLD CHICKEN MOUSSE WITH TOMATO COULIS AND MINT

Chicken mousse is beautiful presented at room temperature with a coulis of fresh tomatoes.

1 Prepare and cook the chicken mousse as directed in the main recipe. Let cool to room temperature.
2 Omit the butter sauce and make a tomato coulis: Peel, seed, and roughly chop ½ lb fresh tomatoes; purée in a food processor until very smooth. With the motor running, gradually add 1 tbsp olive oil to make an emulsion. Season to taste.
3 Unmold the mousse onto individual plates, spoon around the tomato coulis, and sprinkle with shredded fresh mint.

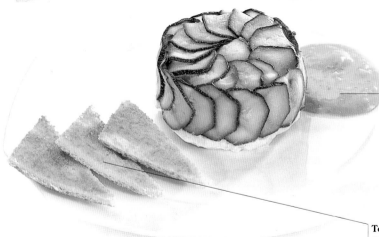

Madeira butter sauce is spooned next to mousse on plate

Toast triangles are recommended accompaniment

CHICKEN POT PIES WITH HERB CRUST

🍽 SERVES 4-6   🥣 WORK TIME 25-35 MINUTES   🍲 COOKING TIME 22-25 MINUTES

EQUIPMENT

chef's knife

wooden spatula

pastry brush

3½-inch cookie cutter

colander   strainer

saucepans

whisk   bowls

2 round-bladed knives*

large metal spoon

4-6 small pot pie dishes, 4½ inches across

chopping board

*rounded pastry cutter can also be used

Everybody has a version of chicken pot pie; mine uses an herbed biscuit crust for the topping. No accompaniments are needed.

GETTING AHEAD

The filling can be prepared 1 day ahead and refrigerated, but mix the biscuit dough just before baking the pies.

SHOPPING LIST

3	medium carrots
3	celery stalks
1	small bunch of parsley
1	medium onion
3	large potatoes, total weight about 1½ lbs
1 quart	chicken stock
1 cup	peas
1	whole cooked chicken, weighing 4 lbs, or 1 lb cooked skinless, boneless chicken
¼ cup	butter
¼ cup	flour
¾ cup	heavy cream
	ground nutmeg
	salt and pepper
1	egg
	For the herb biscuit topping
2 cups	flour
1 tbsp	baking powder
1 tsp	salt
¼ cup	butter
¾ cup	milk, more if needed
1	small bunch of parsley

INGREDIENTS

milk   chicken

carrots

potatoes   egg   onion

peas

parsley

celery stalks

chicken stock

heavy cream

flour

nutmeg   baking powder   butter

ORDER OF WORK

1 MAKE THE FILLING

2 MAKE THE HERB BISCUIT TOPPING

3 ASSEMBLE AND BAKE THE PIES

1 MAKE THE FILLING

1 Slice the carrots. Trim and thinly slice the celery. Chop the parsley. Chop the onion.

2 Square off the sides of the peeled potatoes. Cut each potato vertically into slices. Stack the slices and cut them into even strips of uniform thickness.

3 Gather the strips together into a pile and slice them evenly crosswise to produce medium dice.

4 Heat the stock to boiling in a large saucepan. Add the carrots, potatoes, and celery and simmer 3 minutes.

5 Add the peas and simmer until the vegetables are tender, 5 minutes.

Add well-drained vegetables to chicken meat

6 Drain the vegetables in the colander, reserving the stock. If using a whole chicken, remove the meat from the bones, discarding all skin and any gristle. Cut the meat into slivers and put in a bowl. Add the vegetables.

7 Melt the butter in a small saucepan over medium heat. Add the chopped onion and cook until softened but not browned, 3-5 minutes. Sprinkle the flour over the onions and cook, stirring, 1-2 minutes.

Whisk cream into sauce to enrich it

8 Stir in 2 cups of the stock and heat, whisking, until the sauce comes to a boil and thickens. Simmer 2 minutes, then add the cream and a pinch of nutmeg and taste for seasoning.

9 Pour the sauce over the chicken and vegetables, add the chopped parsley, and mix gently to combine.

2 MAKE THE HERB BISCUIT TOPPING

Add just enough milk to bind mixture to a dough

1 Sift the flour into a large bowl with the baking powder and salt. Make a well in the center. Add the butter and cut it into small pieces using the round-bladed knives.

2 Rub the mixture with your fingertips until it forms fine crumbs, lifting and crumbling to aerate it. Chop the parsley and add it to the flour mixture in bowl.

3 Make a well in the center, add the milk, and cut in quickly with a knife to form coarse crumbs. Add a little more milk if the mixture seems dry.

4 Mix the dough with your fingers just until it comes together. Turn onto a floured surface and knead lightly for a few seconds until smooth.

! TAKE CARE !
Do not overwork the dough or it will be tough.

Knead dough until evenly combined and smooth

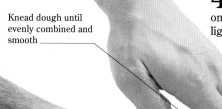

Cut circles close together

ANNE SAYS
"If you don't have a cookie cutter, you can use the top of a large glass to cut out rounds."

5 With your fingers, pat the dough out to ½-inch thickness without stretching it.

6 Cut out rounds with the cookie cutter. Pat out the trimmings and cut additional rounds, for a total of 4-6.

3 ASSEMBLE AND BAKE THE PIES

2 Place a biscuit round on top of each pie. Beat the egg with ½ tsp salt and brush the biscuits with this glaze. Bake the pies for 15 minutes in the heated oven. Reduce the heat to 350°F and continue baking until the crust is browned and the filling is hot, 7-10 minutes.

1 Heat the oven to 425°F. Divide the filling evenly among the small pot pie dishes.

VARIATION
LARGE CHICKEN POT PIE

1 Prepare the filling as directed in the main recipe.
2 Instead of baking the pies in individual dishes, spoon the filling into a medium baking dish.
3 Omit the chopped parsley from the biscuit dough, roll out the dough, and cut into 8 rounds using a 2½-inch cookie cutter.
4 Arrange the rounds over the filling, glaze, and bake, allowing 15 minutes at 425°F and then about 20-25 minutes at 350°F.

Filling should be bubbling hot and give off delicious aroma

Biscuit topping bakes to a rich golden brown

Pot pie dishes look attractive but deep soup bowls can also be used

BROILED BABY CHICKENS WITH MUSHROOM SAUCE

Poussins en Crapaudine Dijonnaise

🍽 SERVES 2   ⏲ WORK TIME 30-40 MINUTES   🍲 COOKING TIME 35-40 MINUTES

EQUIPMENT

- poultry shears
- fork
- shallow dishes
- chef's knife
- 2-pronged fork
- chopping board
- saucepans
- whisk
- paper towels
- wooden spoon
- pastry brush
- 4 metal skewers

INGREDIENTS

- small chickens
- shallots
- mushrooms
- watercress
- white wine vinegar
- dry white wine
- butter
- chicken stock
- Dijon-style mustard
- dry bread crumbs
- garlic clove
- flour

A "crapaud" is a toad, which these small birds resemble after they have been flattened on skewers for broiling. A Cornish hen is the best substitute for a "poussin" (single-serving baby chicken), but a bigger chicken to serve 2 can be used instead. Pungent Dijon mustard flavors the accompanying mushroom sauce.

SHOPPING LIST

2	small chickens, weighing about 1 lb each
	oil for broiler rack
2 tbsp	butter
	salt and pepper
1 tbsp	Dijon-style mustard
2 tbsp	dry bread crumbs
	bunch of watercress for decoration
	For the mushroom sauce
1/4 cup	butter
2 tbsp	flour
5 oz	mushrooms
2	shallots
1	garlic clove
1/4 cup	medium dry white wine
1/4 cup	white wine vinegar
1 1/2 tbsp	Dijon-style mustard, or to taste
1 1/2 cups	chicken stock

ORDER OF WORK

1 SPLIT AND FLATTEN THE CHICKENS

2 COOK THE CHICKENS

3 MAKE THE MUSHROOM SAUCE

1 SPLIT AND FLATTEN THE CHICKENS

1 Set one chicken breast-side down on the board. With the poultry shears, cut along each side of the backbone and discard it.

2 Trim any flaps of skin and cut off the wing tips.

3 Force the bird open and snip the wishbone. Wipe the inside of the bird with paper towels.

4 Turn the bird breast-side up with the legs turned in. With the heel of your hand, push down sharply on the breast to break the breastbone and flatten the bird.

Use one hand to exert more pressure on the other

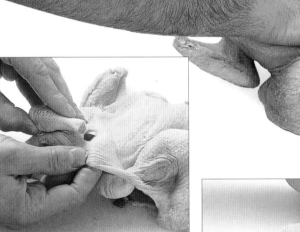

ANNE SAYS

"Small birds that are split and flattened like this remain moist naturally because the bones disperse the heat. If you are substituting a larger chicken, you will need to baste more frequently with melted butter."

5 Make a small cut in the skin between the leg and breastbone and tuck in the leg knuckles.

6 Thread a skewer through the wings of the bird to hold it flat. Thread a second skewer through the legs. Repeat the procedure for the second bird.

COOK THE CHICKENS

1 Heat the broiler. Brush the broiler rack with oil. Melt the butter in a small saucepan. Brush the chickens with half of the melted butter and sprinkle them with salt and pepper.

Apply even coating with pastry brush

Skewers keep chicken flat during cooking

2 Put the chickens on the broiler rack, skin-side up. Broil about 3 inches from the heat, basting once with butter, about 15 minutes.

3 Turn the chickens over with the 2-pronged fork, brush with the remaining butter, and broil 10 minutes on the other side.

4 Turn the chickens over again and brush the skin with the mustard, then sprinkle with the bread crumbs. Broil, skin-side toward the heat, until the birds are tender when pierced with the 2-pronged fork, about 10 minutes longer. While the chickens are cooking, make the sauce.

! TAKE CARE !
If the chickens brown too quickly at any point during cooking, lower the rack further from the heat.

3 MAKE THE MUSHROOM SAUCE

Wipe mushrooms with damp paper towels before slicing

1 In a shallow dish, mash half of the butter with the flour using the fork, until soft. Work the mixture to a paste. Set it aside.

ANNE SAYS
"*The paste should be soft so it will combine easily with the sauce liquid. If necessary, work it with your fingers for a moment so the heat of your hand softens the butter.*"

2 Clean and slice the mushrooms. Finely chop the shallots. Finely chop the garlic.

3 Melt half of the remaining butter in a medium saucepan. Add the mushrooms and cook, stirring occasionally, until tender and lightly browned, 3-5 minutes.

4 Melt the remaining butter in another saucepan, add the shallots and garlic, and cook until softened. Add the wine and vinegar and simmer until reduced to about 2 tbsp.

Add browned mushrooms to mustard sauce and cook a few more minutes

5 Add the mustard and stock and stir to combine.

6 Stir in the cooked mushrooms and simmer 5 minutes.

7 Whisk the flour paste into the simmering sauce, a small piece at a time, until the sauce lightly coats the back of a spoon. Season with salt and pepper to taste.

Add butter and flour paste in small pieces, whisking in just enough to thicken sauce to desired consistency

French fries, the more finely cut the better, are a favorite accompaniment for broiled chicken. The greatest treat is straw potatoes - potatoes cut into matchsticks and deep fried

🍽 TO SERVE

Twist off the stems of watercress, leaving a "bouquet" of sprigs. Remove the skewers from the chickens. Arrange the chickens on individual plates and decorate with watercress. Spoon on a little sauce, serve the rest separately.

—— GETTING AHEAD ——

The sauce can be made up to 3 days ahead and kept, covered, in the refrigerator. The chickens can be prepared early in the day for the evening, but broil them just before serving.

V A R I A T I O N
BROILED CHICKEN WITH GARLIC HERB BUTTER

A larger bird can also be flattened and broiled on skewers as in Broiled Baby Chickens with Mushroom Sauce; the addition of garlic herb butter under the skin helps keep the bird moist, so you may omit the sauce altogether. Serve garnished with fresh chervil or tarragon. For serving, cut up the bird into 4 pieces using a chef's knife and poultry shears.

Garlic herb butter under skin gives attractive appearance to broiled chicken

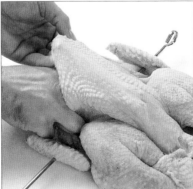

1 Split and flatten a 2½- to 3 lb chicken as directed for the small birds in the main recipe, and insert 2 large skewers to keep it flat.

2 Chop a small bunch each of fresh tarragon and chervil. Finely chop 2 garlic cloves. Using a fork, beat the herbs and garlic into ½ cup softened butter. Season to taste with salt, pepper, and a squeeze of lemon juice.

3 With your fingers, loosen the skin on the chicken breast. Using a small knife, loosen the skin from the top end of the thigh meat, then ease the skin away from the meat with your fingers.

4 Spread about half of the garlic herb butter between the meat and skin of the legs, using your fingers. Spread the rest of the butter on the meat underneath the breast skin.

5 Cook the chicken as directed, omitting the mustard and dry bread crumbs. Allow 20 minutes broiling skin-side up, 15 minutes skin-side down, and a final 10-15 minutes, basting with the pan juices.

COLD CHICKEN AND HAM PIE

 SERVES 8-10   WORK TIME 50-60 MINUTES*   COOKING TIME 1½ HOURS

EQUIPMENT

meat grinder**

kitchen scissors

small frying pan

small knife

pastry brush

chef's knife

boning knife

metal spatula

bowls

rolling pin

grater

aluminum foil

8-9 inch springform pan

medium saucepan

wooden spoon

metal spoon

fork

2 round-bladed knives

shallow dishes

metal skewer

strainer

** food processor can also be used

A typical English pie that I remember well from my childhood. The tasty butter-and-lard crust encases a filling of chicken, hard-boiled eggs, and ham. Wedges of pie are good served with a mixed green salad and with chutney or pickled onions.

GETTING AHEAD

The pie can be made up to 3 days ahead and kept refrigerated, or it can be frozen.

plus 6-8 hours cooling time

SHOPPING LIST

4	skinless, boneless chicken breast halves, total weight about 1½ lbs
¾ lb	lean boneless pork
1	lemon
9	eggs
1 tsp	dried thyme
1 tsp	dried sage
¼ tsp	ground nutmeg
	salt and pepper
¾ lb	cooked lean ham
	butter for pan
	For the pastry dough
4 cups	flour
2 tsp	salt
⅓ cup	butter
⅓ cup	lard
¾ cup	water, more if needed

INGREDIENTS

chicken breast halves

eggs

pork

lemon

ham

butter

lard

dried thyme

ground nutmeg

dried sage

flour

ORDER OF WORK

1 MAKE THE PASTRY DOUGH

2 MAKE THE FILLING

3 LINE THE PAN

4 ASSEMBLE AND BAKE THE PIE

MAKE THE PASTRY DOUGH

ANNE SAYS
"If you have warm hands, which can make the butter soft when rubbing it in, and result in an oily dough, you may prefer to make the dough in a food processor."

1 Sift the flour into a large bowl with the salt using the strainer and make a well in the center.

2 Put the butter and lard in the well and cut them into small pieces using the round-bladed knives.

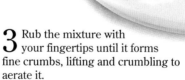

3 Rub the mixture with your fingertips until it forms fine crumbs, lifting and crumbling to aerate it.

Lift your fingers as you rub mixture to incorporate air

4 Make a well in the center, add the water, and mix quickly with a knife to form crumbs. If the mixture seems dry, add 1-2 tbsp more water.

5 Mix the dough together with your fingers; it should be soft but not sticky.

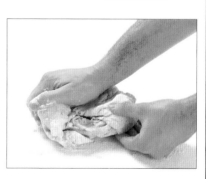

6 Turn the dough onto a floured surface and knead lightly with the heel of the hand for 5-10 seconds until smooth. Wrap the dough and chill 30 minutes in the refrigerator. Meanwhile, make the filling.

2 MAKE THE FILLING

1 Remove the tendon from each chicken breast half. Cut 2 of the chicken breast halves and the pork into chunks; reserve the remaining 2 chicken breast halves.

2 Work the pork and chicken chunks through the fine blade of the meat grinder. Put the ground meats in a large bowl.

ANNE SAYS
"A meat grinder will give a light texture to the stuffing. If you prefer, you can use a food processor, but take care not to purée too finely."

3 Grate the zest from about half of the lemon onto the ground meats in the bowl.

ANNE SAYS
"To remove all the grated lemon zest from the grater, brush it with a stiff brush."

4 With the fork, beat 2 eggs until mixed; add to the ground meats with the thyme, sage, nutmeg, salt, and pepper. Mix well with the wooden spoon, then beat the filling until it pulls from the side of the bowl, 3-5 minutes.

Cut chicken and ham into neat cubes for best appearance

5 To test the mixture for seasoning, fry a little piece in the small frying pan, turning once, and taste – it should be well seasoned, so add more salt and pepper if required.

Add beaten eggs to ground meat mixture, to bind it

6 Cut the reserved chicken breast halves and the ham into ¾-inch cubes. Stir the chicken and ham cubes into the filling mixture.

ANNE SAYS
"To give the finished pie a pretty striped look, the chicken and ham cubes can be spread between the layers of the puréed filling instead of being mixed in. If you prefer to do this, reserve the chicken and ham cubes until step 2 of Assemble and Bake the Pie (see page 116)."

3 LINE THE PAN

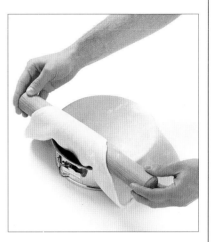

1 Butter the bottom and side of the springform pan.

ANNE SAYS
"You can brush the pan with melted or well-softened butter."

2 Cut off about three-quarters of the dough and shape it into a ball; keep the remaining dough covered. On a floured surface, roll out the ball of dough into a ¼-inch-thick circle that is large enough to line the pan with dough left to overhang. (Test by setting the pan on the dough.)

3 Loosely roll the dough around the rolling pin and unroll it over the prepared pan.

! TAKE CARE !
Do not stretch the dough or it will shrink back during baking.

4 Ease the dough into the pan, pressing it well into the bottom and then against the side. Try to avoid pleats in the side of the dough.

Handle rolled-out dough gently so it doesn't stretch or tear

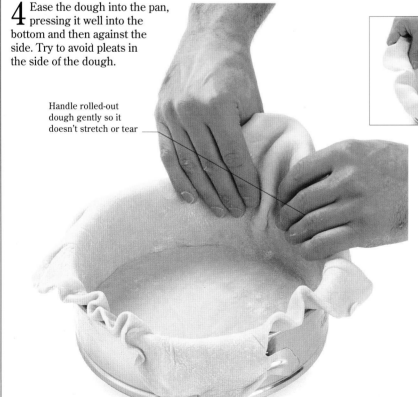

5 Trim the dough edges with scissors, leaving about ½ inch overhanging. Add the trimmings to the remaining dough.

4 ASSEMBLE AND BAKE THE PIE

1 Put 6 eggs in a pan of cold water, bring to a boil, and simmer 10 minutes. Run cold water into the pan to stop the cooking, then let cool. Drain the eggs; tap them on the work surface to crack the shells all over, then peel.

2 Spread half of the filling in the pastry case. Arrange the hard-boiled eggs on top, gently pushing them into the filling. Cover with the remaining filling, ensuring all the gaps are filled.

3 Fold the trimmed dough overhang over the filling. Beat the remaining egg with ½ tsp salt for the glaze. Brush the edge of the dough with egg glaze.

4 Roll out the remaining dough to a circle about ¼-inch thick. Set the pan on top and cut around the base to form a lid of dough the diameter of the pan.

Use base of pan as guide to cut out dough lid; reserve dough trimmings to make decorations for top

5 Lay the dough lid over the filling and press the edges of dough together to seal.

6 Using the skewer, poke a hole in the dough lid and insert a roll of foil to form a chimney so that the steam can escape during baking.

7 Roll out the dough trimmings to ¼-inch thick and cut into strips about 1-inch wide. Cut diagonally across the strips to make leaves. Mark veins on the leaves with the back of the small knife. Curve the leaves with your fingers.

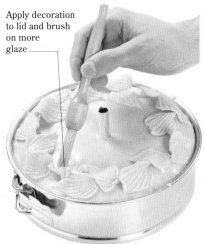

Apply decoration to lid and brush on more glaze

8 Brush the lid with egg glaze. Arrange the leaves on the lid and brush with egg glaze. Chill the pie until firm, about 30 minutes. Meanwhile, heat the oven to 400°F.

🍽 TO SERVE

Unmold the pie and let it come to room temperature. Serve it whole or cut into generous wedges.

9 Bake the pie until golden brown, about 1 hour. Reduce the heat to 350°F and continue baking about 30 minutes longer, until the crust is very brown and the skewer inserted in the stuffing is hot to the touch when withdrawn after 30 seconds. Let the pie cool, then discard the foil chimney, and chill the pie 3-4 hours.

! TAKE CARE !
If the pie is browning too quickly, cover it loosely with foil. If the glaze cracks, brush again with egg just before you lower the oven temperature.

VARIATION

HOT CHICKEN AND HAM PIE

In France, the hard-boiled eggs would be omitted from this pie and it would be served hot as a first course, with this horseradish cream sauce as an accompaniment.

Whip 1 cup heavy cream until stiff and stir in 2-3 tbsp grated fresh horseradish or 3-4 tbsp bottled horseradish. Season the sauce to taste.

SAUTE OF CHICKEN WITH GARLIC AND WINE VINEGAR

Sauté de Poulet au Vinaigre de Vieux Vin

 SERVES 4   WORK TIME 15-20 MINUTES    COOKING TIME 40-50 MINUTES

EQUIPMENT

kitchen string

large sauté pan with lid

saucepan

chef's knife

2-pronged fork

wooden spoon

small ladle

whisk

chopping board

strainer

ANNE SAYS
"Herb and other flavored vinegars can be used in this recipe, each adding its own distinctive taste. When the flavor is concentrated, for example with sherry and balsamic vinegar, you will need only half the amount called for in the recipe."

Another variation on the sauté, this one has a piquant sauce made with red wine vinegar and tomatoes. The amount of garlic might seem excessive, but its flavor mellows as it cooks, and it acts as a thickening agent for the sauce. Sauté potatoes are a rustic French accompaniment.

GETTING AHEAD

The chicken can be sautéed and refrigerated in the sauce, covered, up to 2 days.

SHOPPING LIST

1	chicken, weighing 3-3½ lbs
	salt and pepper
1 tbsp	vegetable oil
6 tbsp	butter
15	garlic cloves
1 cup	red wine vinegar
1 tbsp	tomato paste
2	tomatoes
1	bouquet garni
1 cup	chicken stock

INGREDIENTS

chicken

garlic cloves

tomatoes

tomato paste

butter

chicken stock

bouquet garni

vegetable oil

red wine vinegar

ORDER OF WORK

1 PREPARE AND SAUTE THE CHICKEN

2 MAKE THE GARLIC AND VINEGAR SAUCE

1 PREPARE AND SAUTE THE CHICKEN

1 Cut up the chicken into 6 pieces (see steps 1-4 of How to Cut Up a Chicken into 8 Pieces, page 29). Alternatively, buy a chicken cut up into 6 pieces. Season the pieces with salt and pepper. Heat the oil and 1 tbsp of the butter in the sauté pan over medium heat until foaming. Add the chicken legs, skin-side down, and sauté until they begin to brown, about 5 minutes.

2 Add the breast pieces and continue cooking gently until very brown, about 10-15 minutes. Turn and brown the other side.

3 Add the unpeeled garlic cloves. Shake the pan gently to distribute the garlic in among the chicken pieces, then cover and cook over low heat 20 minutes.

Skins of garlic cloves will be strained out before serving

4 Stir in the vinegar and simmer, uncovered, until reduced by half, about 10 minutes.

Vinegar's acidity is moderated by boiling

5 Add the tomato paste to the pan and stir to mix with the juices in the pan.

6 Coarsely chop the tomatoes. Add the bouquet garni and tomatoes to the pan and mix into the chicken.

Remove chicken pieces as they are cooked and keep warm

7 Cover again and simmer until the chicken pieces are tender when pierced with the 2-pronged fork and the juices run clear, 5-10 minutes longer. If some pieces are done before others, remove them and keep warm.

MAKE THE GARLIC AND VINEGAR SAUCE

Use small ladle to press garlic pulp through strainer with sauce

1 Remove all the chicken pieces from the pan and keep warm. Add the chicken stock to the juices in the pan and boil until well reduced and concentrated in flavor, 3-5 minutes, stirring occasionally.

2 Strain the sauce into the saucepan, pressing hard on the garlic to extract the pulp.

Sautéed potatoes are the traditional accompaniment in Burgundy, where this dish originated

3 Cut the remaining butter into small pieces. Bring the sauce back to a boil, then remove from the heat and add the butter, a few pieces at a time, whisking constantly and moving the pan on and off the heat. Do not boil; the butter should thicken the sauce creamily without melting to oil. Taste for seasoning.

¶◉¶ TO SERVE
Arrange the chicken pieces on individual plates and spoon on the sauce.

Green beans or creamed kidney beans are a good complement to the garlic flavor of the sauce

CHICKEN KNOW-HOW

Chicken lends itself to many different recipes and it is sold in many forms and sizes. Choosing the right bird is important, as is knowing how to store it, whether in the refrigerator or freezer. When it comes to thawing a frozen chicken, care is essential, and the meat must also be carefully handled during preparation.

CHOOSING

You won't find much variety in supermarket chickens, but a couple of rules hold:

• Fresh chicken is preferable to frozen, but a bird that has been frozen quickly, and then correctly handled, should maintain its quality.

• Skin should be light colored and moist; if wet, the chicken probably has been poorly frozen.

• A golden color is not a guide to quality. Yellow skin does not always indicate a cornfed bird but simply the use of yellow foodstuffs.

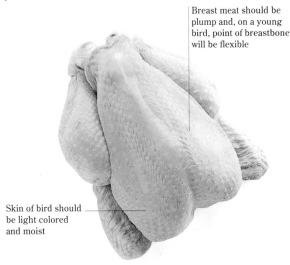

Breast meat should be plump and, on a young bird, point of breastbone will be flexible

Skin of bird should be light colored and moist

A look at the label will reveal some useful information. The U.S. has strict inspection procedures as well as voluntary grading systems. Some butchers also carry free-range chickens that have been fed a grain diet and allowed to roam in the open air. This will be indicated on the label. Free-range chickens are considerably more expensive than ordinary supermarket birds, but many cooks find the superior flavor and texture of free-range chickens make them worth the price.

The label will also give the weight, which is useful when considering cooking methods. Young tender birds are good for broiling, barbecuing, frying, and roasting. Traditionally, the larger the bird, the better the flavor. Fat develops under the skin and in the meat, making it more tender when cooked. However, when buying a large chicken of five pounds or more, be sure it is not too old to roast. Such an old hen is aptly called a boiling fowl because its meat is tough. Poaching or braising will make it tender, while the cooking liquid forms the basis for a rich, full-flavored sauce.

Almost all chickens are sold cleaned with their innards removed. The giblets (neck, gizzard, heart, and liver) are in the cavity, so be sure to remove them. Neck, gizzard, and heart are good for stock (see page 124); the liver can be chopped to flavor a sauce, gravy, or a stuffing.

STORING FRESH CHICKEN

A cleaned, fresh chicken can be kept in the refrigerator for up to two days. Discard any tight plastic wrapping and cover the bird loosely. If wrapped in butcher shop paper, unwrap it, place on a large dish, and cover loosely with waxed paper.

FREEZING

When freezing a whole bird, remove and wrap any giblets separately. If you truss a whole chicken with string before freezing, it will be ready for cooking when thawed. Put the bird in a plastic freezer bag and overwrap it with aluminum foil. Chicken pieces can also be frozen, wrapped first in a layer of plastic wrap, then foil.

Cooked chicken can be frozen with or without bones, but tends to dry out if kept for longer than two weeks. However, when covered with sauce or poaching liquid, it freezes well for up to three months if tightly wrapped.

! TAKE CARE !
Never refreeze raw chicken and do not freeze stuffed birds because the stuffing will not freeze sufficiently to prevent bacteria from developing.

THAWING

It is best to let a chicken thaw in the refrigerator; allow approximately three hours per pound. To speed thawing time, place the bird in its original plastic wrapping in the sink or a large bowl and cover with cold water. Change the water regularly until the chicken thaws. Using this method, a large bird will thaw in three to five hours.

! TAKE CARE !
A frozen bird should be cooked within 12 hours of thawing.

CLEANING AND HANDLING

Do not rinse a chicken before cooking; just wipe out the cavity with a damp paper towel. If the chicken has been frozen, blot the skin with a dry paper towel to absorb as much moisture as possible.

Always wash your hands thoroughly before and after handling raw chicken. Chopping boards, knives, food processors, and other items of kitchen equipment, should be scalded with hot water and thoroughly washed before being used in the preparation of other ingredients. These are preventive measures to destroy possible salmonella bacteria that could contaminate other foods.

STORING COOKED CHICKEN

Chicken should stand no more than an hour at room temperature after cooking. If keeping longer than this, store it loosely wrapped in the refrigerator and use within three days. If the chicken has a strong sauce or stuffing, it should be eaten within 24 hours. Stuffing and gravy can be stored separately in covered containers and reheated just before serving. Be sure the gravy reaches boiling point.

SIZES AND SERVINGS

Chickens are available in many sizes. The servings given are approximate, depending on your appetite and the amount of other ingredients in the recipe.

• Baby chickens (poussins) and small cock birds (coquelets) normally weigh about one pound and serve one person. Other white-fleshed birds, which can be directly substituted for baby chickens, include Rock Cornish hens, which have been bred to serve one or two people.

• Frying, broiling or spring chickens of under three pounds serve two to four people. They can be bought whole or cut in half or pieces.

• Whole roasting chickens over three pounds are more mature, fatter birds, serving four or more people.

SALMONELLA BACTERIA

! TAKE CARE !

Poultry is particularly susceptible to contamination by salmonella bacteria, which causes food poisoning. It is vitally important that chicken be handled and prepared carefully:

• If storing chicken, keep it loosely wrapped in the refrigerator for no more than two days.
• Thaw frozen birds completely before cooking.
• Bring all birds to room temperature before cooking.
• Wash your hands and all equipment before and after handling the raw flesh.
• Stuff the cavity loosely, or do not stuff it at all so that heat penetration kills any salmonella bacteria.
• Cook chicken thoroughly for best flavor and to protect against salmonella. Pieces should fall easily from a two-pronged fork and the juice running from the thigh should be clear. To test a chicken for doneness, lift it up and tip it so the juices run from the cavity – they should be clear not pink.
• Because some microwave ovens produce inadequate cooking temperatures, I do not advocate using a microwave oven for cooking or reheating chicken .

• Large chickens often are sold cut up into pieces. Individual parts also are sold in packages.

• Boiling (sometimes called stewing) chickens are mature hens weighing more than five pounds that serve at least six people. Stewing hens are best with plenty of liquid (braised or poached). A cock, a mature male bird, is found only in country markets and a few specialty stores. The meat is dark, resembling a game bird. A fowl or large roasting chicken is the best alternative.

• Capons are neutered cock birds, very plump and white. They are specially fattened to yield large amounts of breast meat, weigh up to ten pounds, and serve 10 to 12 people.

Baby Chicken

Coquelet

Boiling Chicken

Chicken

Capon

CHICKEN STOCK

Chicken stock is an indispensable ingredient in many sauces and soups. It keeps well up to 3 days, covered, in the refrigerator, and it also freezes well. Stock is often reduced to concentrate for a recipe, so salt and pepper are not added while it is cooking.

🍽 MAKES ABOUT 2 QUARTS

🥣 WORK TIME 15 MINUTES

🍲 COOKING TIME UP TO 3 HOURS

SHOPPING LIST

2-2½ lbs	raw chicken backs and necks, or 1 whole stewing chicken
1	onion
1	carrot
1	celery stalk
1	bouquet garni
5	peppercorns
2 quarts	water, more if needed

1 Put the chicken in a large pot. Quarter the onion, carrot, and celery stalk and add to the pot with the bouquet garni and peppercorns.

2 Add water just to cover the ingredients. Bring to a boil and simmer up to 3 hours, skimming occasionally. If using a stewing chicken, remove it when the thigh is tender when pierced with a skewer, 1¼-1½ hours. It can then be used in a recipe calling for cooked chicken meat.

ANNE SAYS
"The longer the stock simmers, the more flavor it has."

3 Strain the stock into a large bowl. Cool, then cover and keep in the refrigerator.

ANNE SAYS
"If you do not make stock at home, buy good canned broth (preferably low sodium so that you can control seasoning) or use bouillon cubes."

BASIC TECHNIQUES
REMOVING A WISHBONE

Fold back the neck skin of the chicken. With the point of a knife, loosen the wishbone and remove it. Also remove any fat. When the wishbone is removed, breast meat is easy to carve into thin slices.

CUTTING CHICKEN UP INTO 8 PIECES

Using a chef's or boning knife, cut down between the leg joint and body on one side. Twist the bone sharply outward to break the joint, then cut through, and pull the leg from the body. Repeat this procedure for the other leg.

Slit chicken closely along the breastbone to loosen the meat, then split the breastbone with a chef's knife or poultry shears. Turn the bird over and cut the rib bones and backbone from the breast in one piece, leaving the wing joints attached to the breast. The two halves of the bird are now divided into four pieces of meat.

Cut each breast piece in half diagonally, so that some meat is included with the wing bone. Cut off any sharp bones. This makes 6 pieces.

Cut each leg in half through the joint, between the thigh and the drumstick, using the line of fat as a guide. Now there are 8 pieces.

REMOVING A TENDON

Strip the tendon from the center of the breast half by stroking with a boning knife. If the inner fillet becomes detached, replace it. Pull off any skin and discard.

TRUSSING

Wipe the inside of the chicken with paper towels and season with salt and pepper. Remove the wishbone. Set the bird breast up and push the legs back and down. Insert a threaded trussing needle at the knee joint, push through the bird, and out through the other knee joint. Turn the bird back-side up. Pull the neck skin over the neck cavity and tuck the wing tips over it. Push the needle through both sections of one wing into the neck skin, and continue under the backbone to the other side. Push the needle through both wing bones of the second wing. Turn the bird on its side. Pull the ends of the string firmly together and tie securely. Turn the bird breast up. Tuck the tail into the cavity of the bird and fold over the top skin. Push the needle through the skin. Loop the string around one drumstick, under the breastbone, and over the other drumstick. Tie the ends of the string together.

CARVING

Remove the trussing string. With a carving or chef's knife, cut down between the leg and the body. Turn the bird on its side and cut around the oyster meat so it remains attached to the thigh. Turn the bird on its back. Twist the leg sharply outward to break the joint, then cut through the joint and pull the leg from the body. Repeat the procedure for the other leg. Halve the leg by cutting through the joint, using the line of white fat as a guide. Cut horizontally above the wing joint, through to the breastbone, so you can carve a complete slice of breast meat. Carve the breast in slices parallel to the rib cage. Cut off the wing. Carve the other side in the same way.

BONING COOKED CHICKEN

Using a boning knife, cut down between the leg and body joints. Twist the leg sharply outward to break the joint, then cut through the joint and pull the leg from the body. Repeat for the other leg. Slit along one side of the chicken breastbone. Using your fingers and the point of the knife, loosen the breast meat from the carcass, removing the breast half in one piece. Repeat for the other breast. Pull away the wishbone and the meat adhering to it. Pull off any remaining meat from the carcass. Pull off the skin from the pieces and discard. Shred the meat with your fingers and pile on a plate. Using your fingers and the point of the knife, tear and cut the meat from the leg bones. Trim away the tendons, discard the skin and shred the meat. Produces about 3 cups.

HOW-TO BOXES

There are pictures of all preparation steps for each **Chicken Classics** *recipe. Some basic techniques are used in a number of recipes; they are shown in extra detail in these special "how-to" boxes:*

INDEX

ACKNOWLEDGMENTS

Photographer David Murray
Photographer's Assistant Jules Selmes

Chef Eric Treuille
Cookery Consultant Linda Collister
Home Economist Annie Nicholls

US Editor Jeanette Mall
Indexer Sally Poole

Typesetting Rowena Feeny
Text film by Disc To Print (UK) Limited

Production Consultant Lorraine Baird

*Anne Willan would like to thank her
chief editor Cynthia Nims and associate
editor Kate Krader for their vital help
with writing the book and researching
and testing the recipes, aided by
La Varenne's chefs and trainees.*